Equip

Building Student Leaders.
Multiplying Disciples.

www.EquipStudentLeaders.com

EQUIP
Building Student Leaders.
Multiplying Disciples.

By Nathan Wilder and Jon Kragel
© Copyright 2013 Nathan Wilder and Jon Kragel.
All rights reserved.

ISBN: 978-1-935986-59-1

LIBERTY
UNIVERSITY.
Press

Lynchburg, VA
www.liberty.edu/LibertyUniversityPress

DEDICATIONS

Nathan Wilder:
I want to thank my beautiful wife, Amber and my four amazing kids, Reese, Macey, Lexie, and Daisy for their full support. I love you guys like crazy!! I dedicate this book to my family as well as all of the students who are leading this generation closer to Jesus!

Jon Kragel:
To my incredible wife, Samantha, and to my two little guys, Jackson and Carter. The three of you teach me more about leadership than the rest of the world combined. In Christ, you are my greatest joy in this life! I love you!

TABLE OF CONTENTS

Find Teaching/Student Outlines, supporting resources,
and author contact information at
www.EquipStudentLeaders.com.

FOREWORD

Through the years, I have been motivated in my quest to
raise up the next generation of leaders by two great thoughts.
First of all, am I content to be one of the multitudes who
merely wrings my hands with fear and complaints about the
future? Or will I be one of those who helps create the future?
Second of all, whoever wants this generation the most will
get them.

As President and Founder of Student Leadership University,
I believe that leadership is a process, not an event. And even
though our various student leadership programs are events
that happen, we know there must be a strong process in
place to allow a student to grow and mature. I also believe
that leaders are not made in a day, but they are made daily.
Therefore, one of the most effective tools in the process
of daily creating student leaders is an effective curriculum
crafted by innovative and experienced youth communicators
and strategists.

If you are a youth pastor, an educator, a student director, or a student teacher, Equip – which is a curriculum designed to help you build your student leadership team – is a must for you. Nathan Wilder and Jon Kragel are two such individuals who have proven themselves very effective in not only reaching and keeping students, but in developing leaders. I've known these two dynamic influencers for many years. I've been in their church, I've worked with their adult teams, and most of all I've met their students throughout the years. What impresses me the most, is that their students have a hunger to be devoted, passionate followers of Jesus but also to continue to grow in effective service to others.

If you are looking for a curriculum to help you motivate, train, and most of all help you have fruit that remains, I would definitely make Equip part of my basic tool kit in changing the lives of impressionable young men and young women.

- Dr. Jay Strack,
President and Founder of Student Leadership University

PREFACE

Who is the greatest ministry leader of all time? No, there's
no trick answer here. Even a young child could give this
standard Sunday School answer... Jesus! Now, if Jesus chose
to invest in twelve leaders to further His Father's Kingdom,
shouldn't we take the time to invest in our student leaders as
well? The advancement of the Christian faith rested on the
shoulders of Christ's leadership team. Likewise, we believe
the advancement of your student ministry rests on the
shoulders of your student leaders. Whether you're a youth
pastor, student director, small group teacher, or parent of a
teenager, you must ask yourself these questions: how are you
preparing your students to lead both today and tomorrow?
How are you keeping their hearts and minds focused on the
Gospel? If there is no student leadership team, where and
how do you begin to form one? Once a leadership team is up
and running, how do you make the team stronger? How can
you engage students with real world leadership and apply it
to student leadership within your ministry?

This book is designed to build student leaders. It is to
be an all-inclusive book of information that will provide
the youth leader with the necessary resources to mentor
student leaders. The team will be trained to learn biblical
foundations, memorize Gospel verses, work through practical
leadership lessons, be motivated by proven leaders, and
complete team building exercises. When the curriculum
is completed, students will be challenged to hold on to
this information and use it as a tool to mentor others. The
idea behind this book is simple: disciple students with
resources they get to keep so that they can turn around and
disciple others.

ENDORSEMENTS

We currently use this curriculum to disciple our eighth grade student leadership team, and over the past seven years we've seen hundreds of students complete the training and apply it within our ministry. Developing student leaders has radically transformed our ministry, expanded our mission, and increased our reach into our community. It is our prayer that this resource will help you do the same. But don't simply take our word for it.

Brent Crowe is the Vice President of Student Leadership University, which has trained over 50,000 students from across the country to become leaders of the Christian faith. He also speaks to tens of thousands of people every year as a preacher and evangelist. Regarding this resource, Brent says the following:

> *"My friends, Nathan Wilder and Jon Kragel, have created a template with Equip for building, investing, equipping, and multiplying a student leadership team. This resource can be used in a youth group of 15 or 150 to raise up a generation who leads at the feet of Jesus. More importantly, Equip communicates one fundamental and often overlooked truth about leadership development...cultivating influence for the glory of God is part of the discipleship process."*

Youth leaders from around the country are already using Equip and seeing great results! Check out what they are saying...

The Equip material has served as a great roadmap for the leadership team. It provides some great biblical teaching as well as solid leadership material to help the students develop both spiritually and functionally. It provides a great foundational structure with which to work off of. You can focus your planning time on finding ways to help the students apply what they're learning.

Chad Moore
Middle School Minister
Shandon Baptist Church
Columbia, South Carolina

Equip is a powerful, scripture-based resource for establishing a dynamic and Christ focused student leadership team. Investing in a student leadership team is an essential component to a healthy and effective youth group because it encourages hands-on experience through planning, decision making, communicating, and working as a team.

Tyler Core
Middle School Minister
First Baptist Church Trussville
Birmingham, Alabama

Equip is a perfect tool for training students on biblical leadership concepts. It combines both biblical concepts and practical leadership training.

Todd Breiner
Middle School Minister/Online Pastor
Christ Fellowship Miami
Miami, Florida

I am a huge advocate for student leadership and have personally used Equip. This is an amazing curriculum. It will give your adult leaders the tools they need to develop your student leaders. It will take your ministry to the next level! Using Equip not only affects the student leaders, but the ministry as a whole.

Melissa Clark
Director of Student Ministries
Fort Mitchell Baptist Church
Fort Mitchell, Kentucky

Equip is greatly beneficial, easy to implement and communicate!

Jeff Lehmen
Discipleship Pastor
First Baptist Church Kissimmee
Kissimmee, Florida

Equip is a foundational study for the Christian life. It brings students to a place where they can confidently love and serve God and others. Equipping students to share their faith and serve, along with providing very practical ways to lead has had an incredible impact on the students I serve. Equip helps lead students to do these very things.

Brian Katauskas
Student Ministries Minister
Northland. A Church Distributed
Longwood, Florida

We pray that God will bless your efforts in impacting the leaders of today and tomorrow. If you are interested in obtaining further resources (such as teacher and student fill-in-the-blank guides for each lesson, sample student leadership applications, and additional leadership exercises), please visit **www.EquipStudentLeaders.com**.

WHY B.U.I.L.D. STUDENT LEADERS?

Bill Hull, in his book, The Disciple Making Church, defines discipleship as "the process that involves life-changing learning in the context of relationships that leads to Christlikeness." His definition includes four key elements to making disciples. First, he acknowledges that discipleship is a process. It is ongoing. According to the contract we signed when we got saved, we're called to follow Christ for at least thirty years, although there's room to refinance after ten... Oh wait, that's not right! We're actually called to follow after Christ for the rest of our lives. We're called to live for Him until He brings us to Heaven or until He returns physically to Earth. And if discipleship is a process, then we must remember that one program won't change the world. However, we believe that if we're able to place right the tools in the right people's hands and create environments that inspire others, we just might change somebody's world. Second, Hull refers to life-changing learning because lessons unapplied equate to lessons never learned in the first place. As James 1:22 reminds us, we must not simply hear the Word of God, but do and live out the Word of God. Third, discipleship always takes place in the context of relationships, as Christ modeled with his twelve disciples. Finally, the end goal of discipleship as mentioned in the definition above is Christ Himself. Paul reminds us in Philippians 3:14 that we should "press on toward the goal for the prize of the upward call of God in Christ Jesus."

Preacher Matt Carter once pointed out that in pursuit of our calling for Christ, we must not forget our calling to Christ. If we pursue our calling to Christ, He'll show us our calling for Him. However, if we only pursue our calling for Christ, we often will miss out on both. Jo Saxon, a current leader in the church planting movement, once stated, "If you try to build the church, you rarely get disciples, but if you try to make disciples you always get the church." Of the 270 occurrences of the word 'disciple' in the Gospels and Acts, never once is the word used to set apart more devout believers from run-of-the-mill believers. True discipleship involves making daily decisions to take up our cross and follow Him, and this is exactly what we're called to do in the Great Commission (Matthew 28:16-20).

LEADERSHIP AND DISCIPLESHIP ARE BEST FRIENDS

Leadership training in the church and discipleship go hand in hand. The true disciples of Jesus Christ became the leaders of the early church movement. John Maxwell has been famously quoted saying, "Everything rises and falls on leadership." Think about it, Jesus placed the future of his ministry in the hands of His disciples. How could Jesus have such confidence in His disciples, who made repeated mistakes, and often missed the point of Jesus' messages? How could Jesus proclaim in John 14:12 that the disciples were going to do greater things than He? Jesus had such confidence and made such assertions for two reasons. First, He knew the power of the Holy Spirit was coming to dwell within the hearts of His believers (John 14:16). While Moses and other Old Testament prophets had the Spirit of God on them, and Jesus spent time in the Gospels with the disciples, it was actually to their benefit in that Jesus was leaving them (John 16:7) because the power of God was coming to live in them! Paul showed evidence of this truth when he claimed in Philippians 4:13, "I can do all things through Him who strengthens me."

Second, Jesus had confidence in His disciples because He had shown them the best example for how to share and spread the Gospel. He gave them a template to use and reach the next generation. We see this truth play out in Acts 6 and 7, where the disciples pass the torch to the next set of leaders to carry on the message of Jesus Christ. Stephen, the first martyr, was not one of the original disciples, but rather he was one who was trained to lead by the disciples. Here we stand two thousand years later, and while the Church is filled with troubles and problems, we can be encouraged that there are more Christians today across the world than at any point in history. Christ's message of hope, forgiveness, salvation, and redemption is alive like never before! If we want to be a part of the movement of God, then we must prepare the way for the next generation through making disciples and training students to be leaders!

While many different definitions of leadership exist in the world today, the definition we use with our students comes from our class notes obtained at Liberty Baptist Theological Seminary. We like the following definition of leadership for its practicality, teachability, and direct parallel to Bill Hull's definition of discipleship given at the beginning of this chapter:

> *Leadership is the process of influencing others to work together for a common purpose or goal.*

Like discipleship, this definition of leadership contains four key elements. First, leadership is a process because leadership involves movement. One can only lead if he or she is going somewhere. Second, leadership involves influence because if no one is following, then whom are you leading? Also, we like the idea of influence being the goal of leadership because influence can take place at any level. You can influence those above you, influence those around you, and influence those who look up to you. Influence involves daily decision-making that shows attitude reflected through action. Leadership means that each day matters and that the means is just as important as the end. Third, leadership involves cooperation because there are certain things in life you cannot do alone. For example, you can't play hide and seek, tag, or marco polo by yourself. It would be kind of awkward if you showed up to a wedding to find out that the bride and groom were the same person. There are certain things in life that you cannot do alone, and the Christian life is one of them. We're called the body of Christ for a reason (1 Corinthians 12:27). Finally, leadership involves having a common purpose because teams work best together when they share a common goal. Sports teams function best when they share the goal of winning the championship. Musicians function best when they play different parts to the same song. Militaries function best when soldiers follow orders to obtain the objective and to ultimately win the war. We believe churches should be able to work through a variety of internal conflicts as long as they keep focus on the goal for the church: we're called to give God glory (1 Corinthians 10:31) through living out the Great Commission (Matthew 28:16-20) and Great Commandments (Matthew 22:36-40).

HOW TO B.U.I.L.D. YOUR LEADERSHIP TEAM

Now that we've established the need for making disciples
through growing student leaders, how can one B.U.I.L.D.
better student leadership teams? The remainder of this book
contains twelve lessons that are designed to do just that.
Each session contains the following five elements:

1 Boost Biblical Foundations

2 Understand Gospel Verses

3 Improve Leadership Skills

4 Learn Leadership Principles

5 Develop Team Unity

1 *BOOST BIBLICAL FOUNDATIONS*

In order to have biblical leaders, we must know and live by
biblical truths. In this book, you'll be able to walk through six
foundations of the faith, broken down into twelve practical
lessons. First, we take a look at God's faithfulness as the
foundation for Christianity. Second, we teach students how to
seek God on a daily basis, including how to study their Bibles
and how to pray. Third, we discuss the importance of having
a Christian worldview, which gives you a lens through which
to see the culture around you. Next, we instill in the students
the need for a lifestyle defined by love. After this session, we
move to a lesson that shows how attitude affects every area
of our life. We try to teach students how to face life's stressful
times as well as successful times. Finally, we describe to the
student the value of God's holiness and how we're called to
become more like Him with the everyday choices we make.
On top of God's foundation of faithfulness, we truly believe

that students can stand strong and grow fast to become the disciples and leaders of the next generation if they SEEK, SUBMIT, SURROUND, SURRENDER, and STRIVE!

—✕—

② *UNDERSTAND GOSPEL VERSES*

The Bible tells us to meditate on God's Word day and night (Psalm 1:2) and that the renewal of our minds leads to life transformation (Romans 12:2). One of the best ways for us to renew our minds daily is to memorize Scripture. With each lesson in this book, we give one practical Gospel verse, useful for understanding what Christ did for us. While there are many great verses in the Bible to memorize, we wanted to pick twelve verses to teach students the practice of learning God's Word on a personal and practical level. We are called to always be prepared to give a reason for the hope found within us (1 Peter 3:15), and memorizing Gospel verses ensures that we'll have a biblical answer to give those who ask us to explain our faith.

—✕—

③ *IMPROVE LEADERSHIP SKILLS*

No matter where we are in life, we can always stand to improve our leadership skills. The better leaders we train, the more effective disciple-makers we develop. Each lesson in this book includes a real life leadership lesson, designed to get students to think about what, why, and how we do things. This section doesn't simply give them fish, but rather teaches the students intellectually how to fish. Each lesson can be incorporated into a training session or small group Bible study in only five to ten minutes, and all the needed resources for the activity are included in the book. We've seen great discussion and development take place through this part of the training. Improving leadership skills helps students connect the dots between biblical truths and real life application of those truths.

—✕—

4 *LEARN LEADERSHIP PRINCIPLES*

While it is often easier to point out the mistakes of the leaders before us, we must recognize that leadership is a bigger endeavor than simply our ministry or group. Each lesson in this book includes direct quotes from proven leaders to teach specific leadership principles. By using quotes from proven leaders in your teaching sessions, you demonstrate the value of good leadership in a variety of settings, as well as increase the chances that students will remember and apply your lesson in a real life setting. For clarification, using a quote from a leader does not necessarily mean we advocate everything that person teaches or stands for, but rather the quote is meant to enhance the leadership principles we are trying to impart to the students. Each quote also includes a quick description of what that person has done to establish their credibility and deepen the impact of what they are saying. For example, a quote from Steve Jobs on the importance of technology in business should carry more weight for an audience than a quote on the same topic from Steve Johnson, the local coffee shop barista.

—✕—

5 *DEVELOP TEAM UNITY*

The final section of each lesson includes a team building exercise, designed specifically to help unify the group whom you are teaching. Bob Russell, in his book, When

God Builds a Church, shares an interesting illustration on the importance of team unity. Have you ever seen the giant redwood trees in California? Do you know which trees I am talking about? The redwood trees are the ones that have trunks the size of houses, and they've stood in their majestic beauty for centuries. One would think these trees would have massive and deep root systems, wouldn't you? However, their roots are few, and they do not go very deep into the ground. If these beautiful trees do not have complex root systems, how then have they managed to last for hundreds of years? Well, the roots of redwood trees actually interweave together, so that when storms roll in, they literally hold each other up. Isn't that a great picture of what the Church should be? A team functions best when everyone's lives are woven together, and these team building exercises help students develop joyful fellowship and relationship with each other.

Remember, each lesson is designed to help you B.U.I.L.D. better student leaders. For more resources, please visit www.EquipStudentLeaders.com.

FOUNDATION OF FAITHFULNESS...
GOD KEEPS HIS PROMISES (PART I)

1 *BOOST BIBLICAL FOUNDATIONS:*

There are many words that describe and define faithfulness.

Faithful: worthy of trust, honest, loyal, reliable, dependable, true, exact, direct, straightforward, trustworthy, devoted, dedicated, consistent, steadfast, unfailing...

Have you ever doubted God's faithfulness? Have you ever wondered if He's really watching over you, or if He's just letting things happen to you for no reason? I know I have. That's the human thing to do. In a world of instants-instant macaroni, instant entertainment, and instant messaging — we expect God to give us instant answers. Although our "spiritual boot camp" is geared towards steady spiritual growth, it's important to recognize that our foundation is Christ alone, and He is always faithful to His promises. In other words, no matter what we're going through, He's got our backs.

Today, I'm going to give you four ways you can know that God is faithful.

ONE: God CLAIMS that He is faithful.

Read the following verses (NIV) and take note of where God claims that He is faithful.

1. Psalm 33:4   *For the word of the Lord is right and true; He is faithful in all he does.*

2. Psalm 36:5   *Your love, O Lord reaches to the heavens, your faithfulness to the skies.*

3. 1 Corinthians 1:9 *God, who has called you into fellowship with His Son Jesus Christ our Lord, is faithful.*

4. Hebrews 10:23   *Let us hold unswervingly to the hope that we profess, for He who promised is faithful.*

Latch on to this FACT: God's Word is binding…we can trust the Bible.

1. God is all-powerful and truthful. If He didn't do what He claimed, He'd be a liar, which would make Him not truthful, and therefore, not God.

2. If you ever doubt the power of God's Word, remember He spoke the world into existence. That's pretty powerful if you ask me!

Have you ever discussed a controversial subject with a small group of your friends? Chances are, not everyone agreed with your personal view point! Do the guests of a typical television talk show ever agree? Very rarely! In contrast, 40 different men wrote the 66 books of the Bible and discussed hundreds of controversial subjects, YET THEY ALL AGREE! What makes this even more remarkable is that the 40 Bible writers lived as much as 1,600 years apart. Imagine their cultural differences!

Despite this great potential for contradiction between writers in the Bible, there is harmony and unity in the Bible's message. That is because the Holy Spirit was directly guiding each of the 40 men who wrote the Bible. One scholar has noted that the unity found in the Bible is vastly superior to the sacred writings of all other world religions, including Buddhism, Zoroastrianism, Bahai, and Islam. Anyone who has ever studied these writings must admit they are jumbles of disjointed material, without order, continuity or unity of any kind. The 66 books of the Bible, on the other hand, weave a UNIFIED message from beginning to end— one theme from Genesis to Revelation. The bottom line is that the CLAIMS and the CONSISTENCY of God's Word prove that He is FAITHFUL to His promises.

TWO: God has proven His faithfulness to His people.

In the following three examples of God proving His FAITHFULNESS to His people, fill in the blanks for:

    a. What makes sense
       (logical from the human perspective)?
    b. What makes no sense
       (not logical from the human perspective)?
    c. What makes "God sense"
       (logical from God's perspective)?
    d. What leaves us in "Awe sense"
       (God proving His faithfulness when it is humanly impossible...which leaves us in awe of Him)?

EXAMPLE 1: Moses— God parted the Red Sea. (Exodus 14 and 15)

    a. What makes sense? Read Exodus 14:10-12.

It would make sense for the Israelites to continue to serve and submit to the Egyptians (at least they were kept alive). It made sense that they desired to escape from Egypt when they continued to get mistreated. So, this is what they did. The Israelites left Egypt, but the Egyptians ran after them with the hopes of recapturing them.

    b. What makes no sense? Read Exodus 14:13-18.

The Israelites' backs were up against the wall. On one side of them, the Egyptians were running towards them and on the other side was the Red Sea! The Egyptians had the Israelites trapped. What would you do in this situation? I would probably jump into the Red Sea and start swimming! It did not makes sense, or seem logical, humanly speaking, for the Israelites to just sit there, to be still, and to trust God when the Egyptians had them cornered.

    c. What makes God sense? Read Exodus 14:21-30.

You see, miracles make sense to God, but not to us. God has the power to make supernatural things happen (things that are extraordinary). Israel chose to stray away from human logic (to run and jump into the Red Sea in the hopes of escaping) and trust in the power of God!

    d. What makes awe sense? Read 14:31-15:21.

The Israelites had to be nervous when the Egyptians had them cornered and were getting closer and closer. But, they trusted God to keep His promise and God was FAITHFUL to His promise! When the Israelites saw the Red Sea part, walked through, and saw the Red Sea crash down on the Egyptians, they were left in awe of God! It was difficult for them to find words to express how awesome God was for performing a miracle. God's FAITHFULNESS showed up in an undeniable way to the Israelites!

EXAMPLE 2: David— God defeated Goliath. (1 Samuel 17)

    a. What makes sense? Read 1 Samuel 17:1-16.

Humanly, it makes sense for David and the Israelites to let Goliath and the Philistines continue to intimidate them and run away. They were much too powerful. Many Israelites would lose their lives if they challenged Goliath.

    b. What makes no sense? Read 1 Samuel 17:32.

It did not make sense for David to make a challenge to fight Goliath. All the odds were against him. It would be like a 6th grader challenging Incredible Hulk to a fight. Take a look at the comparisons!

Goliath: 9 feet tall (many men only reached his waist)
                Coat— 5000 shekels (over 100 pounds)
                Iron point of spear— 600 shekels
                (15 pounds)
                Experienced fighter
                Leader of an army
                Support of a powerful army

David: Young and much smaller than Goliath
                Not well known, a shepherd, not a soldier
                No experience as a fighter in battle
                No armor
                Entire army was scared

c. What makes God sense? Read 1 Samuel 17:37.

Although all odds were against David, he beat Goliath! God
is FAITHFUL to His promise to David.

d. What makes awe sense? Read Psalm 66:1-12.

It's possible that David could have had his battle with
Goliath in mind as he writes these type of Psalms. The
victory over Goliath was a marking moment in David's life.
God proved to David that He is: a FAITHFUL God.

EXAMPLE 3: Peter— God allowed him to walk on water.
(Matthew 14:22-36)

a. What makes sense? Read Matthew 14:26.

It makes sense that Peter and the disciples must be dreaming
or must have foggy vision because humans cannot walk on
water!

b. What makes no sense? Read Matthew 14:29.

It does not make sense for Peter to step off of the boat and
walk toward Jesus. It does not make sense to walk on water!
When is the last time that you walked on water?

c. What makes God sense? Read Matthew 14:29 &31.

Jesus tells Peter to come to Him by walking on the water with
the knowledge that Jesus will sustain him. Jesus kept His
promise as Peter kept his eyes on Him. This is another great
example of God using His supernatural power.

d. What makes awe sense? Read Matthew 14:32-33.

After witnessing Peter walking on the water toward Jesus, the disciples were in awe of Jesus and worshiped Him. God again proved Himself FAITHFUL!

—✕—

❷ *UNDERSTAND GOSPEL VERSES:*

John 1:12 (NIV)– *Yet to all who received Him, to those who believed in His name, He gave the right to become children of God.*

—✕—

❸ *IMPROVE LEADERSHIP SKILLS:*

Process ministry works like Proactiv Solution.

Pass out the attached Proactiv Solution worksheet (Located in the Further Resources). Tell the students to read the "A Revolutionary Treatment: Combination Therapy" section. Ask the students to find similarities between the process of how Proactiv Solution works and how process ministry can work. Help the students see the 3 steps involved in "Combination Therapy" and identify the unique purpose for each step.

How Proactiv Solution works:

Proactiv Solution successfully uses a process called "Combination Therapy" to fight against acne. "Combination Therapy" requires only 3 steps (take note that there are only 3 steps and not 25!). Each step has a specific function or purpose that is unique. Each step is dependent on the other steps. When each step fulfills its purpose and the 3 steps are completed, the fight against acne is victorious!

How Process ministry works:

Process ministry works just like Proactiv Solution. A student ministry should have a 3-4 step spiritual growth process that is modeled with their ministry environments. Each ministry environment should have a specific purpose that is unique. Each ministry environment is dependent on the other ministry environments. When each student moves through the 3-4 ministry environments weekly and brings friends through as well, the fight against Satan is victorious!

Process ministry example:

Environment 1:

Student Worship Service
Purpose: To EXPOSE a student to a relationship
               with Jesus.
               * All energy attempts to fulfill the purpose of
               sharing the Gospel.

Environment 2:

Student Small Groups
Purpose: To EQUIP a student to follow Jesus..
               * All energy attempts to fulfill the purpose of
               spiritually equipping the students.

Environment 3:

Student Ministry Teams
Purpose: To EXPERIENCE life serving Jesus.
               * All energy attempts to create opportunities
               for students to regularly serve the church and
               the community with their spiritual gifts and
               talents.

Application:

Challenge the students to put on their spiritual proactive SOLUTION! Weekly, it is effective to move students through these ministry environments. This is a model of what we should be doing daily. So, challenge the students to share Jesus, have their quiet times with Jesus, and serve in the name of Jesus every day this week.

Further Resources:

Simple Church, by Thom Rainer and Eric Geiger.
Simple Student Ministry, by Eric Geiger and Jeff Borton.

—✕—

4 LEARN LEADERSHIP PRINCIPLES:

"Without faith, nothing is possible.
With it, nothing is impossible."

– McLeod Bethune
(Educator, Author, and African
American Civil Rights Leader)

—✕—

5 DEVELOP TEAM UNITY:

Connect 4:

Bring some Connect 4 games in and allow the students some time to play each other.

Divide the students into groups of four and tell them to learn four new things about each of the four students in their group. When all of the groups are finished, have each person in the group share as many facts that they learned about their group members as possible. By the end of this exercise, the team members should know a lot more about each other!

Application:

Challenge the students to play "Connect 4" each week at your student ministry programs and events. Tell them to meet four new people and learn four facts about their new friends and then give a report on their research the next time you get together. Explain how this outreach effort will not only allow them to meet new people, but it will make the new people feel very welcomed!

FOUNDATION OF FAITHFULNESS...GOD KEEPS HIS PROMISES (PART II)

1 *BOOST BIBLICAL FOUNDATIONS:*

In the previous session, we learned that God proved His faithfulness by claiming it in His Word as well as through His people. In this session, we pick up where we left off and observe the third and fourth ways that God proves Himself faithful.

THREE: God has proven His faithfulness through His prophecies (which are specific predictions) about His Son, Jesus.

Think about this for a second: if God is not faithful on just one promise, then He can't be trusted on any promises. When God makes a promise, He means business. When God spoke through His prophets, He had to be accurate. In fact, if a prophet made a prediction and was wrong, then his life could be taken from him.

Imagine that you are looking to buy a car. The car dealer brings you out to the car of your dreams! It's beautiful. You can't wait to sign off on the paper work, but the dealer says one last thing that completely throws you for a loop. He says that the brakes work 95 percent of the time. Even though the car is beautiful, could you trust it with your life? There is no way that I would purchase a car that has brakes that work 95 percent of the time!

One time, while coming home from a student mission trip, our church shuttle's brakes went out. Thankfully, we had a crafty driver who managed to bring the vehicle to a stop without putting anyone in harm's way. Everyone got off the shuttle so we could try to figure out what happened and decide what to do next. Now, the shuttle brakes had worked up to that point, so why should I be worried that they didn't work that one time? With that reasoning in mind, I loaded everyone back onto the shuttle and we continued on our way home... NO WAY! I couldn't risk the lives of my students on a shuttle whose brakes I couldn't trust! We ended up waiting for several hours for different transportation to come and pick us up, because I couldn't trust a shuttle that's brakes worked only 95 percent of the time. I wouldn't serve a God that was faithful 95 percent of the time either!

Well, you can be confident that God is faithful 100 percent of the time! Another way that He proves His faithfulness is by the predictions He makes about His Son, Jesus.

This is so amazing to me! God made promises about Jesus through His prophets, and hundreds of years later they came true. Follow me on this illustration to help you understand how amazing this is:

Picture the state of Texas. Now, fill the state of Texas up with quarters. That's right, the whole state! Keep filling it up until the quarters are one foot deep. Okay, I'm going to blindfold you. Now, I am going to toss a red quarter somewhere in the middle of all of the other quarters. Your job is to find this quarter. You only have one chance.

What are the chances that you are going to find the red quarter? It is highly unlikely - no, it is next to impossible that you will find the red quarter. This is the same possibility that just 8 predictions about Jesus would come true! Just like finding the red quarter is next to impossible, so are the 8 predictions about Jesus. But, that's not all! There are over

150 predictions about Jesus that were made and came true! Our human minds can't comprehend this. The only way to explain this is to admit that God is a faithful God!

The following are 3 examples of predictions that were made about Jesus and hundreds of years later came true:

	Prediction Made:	Prediction Accounted:
Born of a virgin	Isaiah 7:14	Matthew 1:18-25
Wounded and bruised	Isaiah 53:4-6	1 Peter 2:21-25
Raised from the dead	Psalm 16:8-11	Acts 2:24-31

FOUR: God has proven His faithfulness in your life.

Take a look at the following story about how God proved faithful in a diver's life:

A young man was training for the Olympics as a diver. He did not believe in God, and centered his life on competition. He did have one Christian friend who regularly shared the good news of Jesus Christ with him, but he had never truly given God's message any serious consideration. One night, the diver went to the indoor pool at the local university. The lights were out, but the moonlight shone through the glass windows enough for the diver to feel comfortable to begin his training regiment. He climbed up to the highest diving board, went to the very edge, turned his back to the pool, and extended his arms to the side in preparation to jump. Just then, he saw his shadow on the wall, which was in the shape of a cross. Instead of diving, he knelt down and finally asked Jesus to come into his life. As he stood back up, a maintenance man walked into the room and flipped on the lights. The diver gasped in horror as the pool had been drained for repairs! Although you might not have experienced something as crazy as that diver did, I can promise you that God is faithful.

God has proven faithful many times in each of our lives. Often we don't even notice. Too often we treat God like the wallpaper in our bathroom. How many of you have wallpaper in your bathroom? How many of you can honestly tell me what the pattern is on that wallpaper? Really? I mean, you spend time in there every day and you can't even tell me what the pattern is. Since you don't recognize it, the wallpaper must not exist, right? Wrong.

Here's another test. How many of you are wearing watches right now? Without looking, does your watch (unless it's digital) have tick marks or numbers? You see, just because you don't see God working in your life, doesn't mean He's not. Think about the times where you've been in a scary, tough, challenging, or tempting situation, and God has provided a way out. Think about the times where God brought you comfort, courage, peace, or strength right at the moment you needed it. It would be hard to judge God's existence and faithfulness solely on your experiences, but when you put them with God's claims, His works in the Bible, His prophecies fulfilled, and His promises to us, you can be sure that God will always be faithful to His purposes and plans.

Have you ever flown in an airplane? When you got on the plane, you asked to speak with the pilot, right? No? You mean to tell me that you sat in a two thousand ton tube of metal, went twenty thousand feet in the air with your sole comfort being that your seat turns into a flotation device, and you never asked to speak to the pilot! I confess, I've never asked to see the pilot either, but how can we entrust our lives so easily to earthly pilots we've never met, but be hesitant to trust God, our heavenly pilot? You see, if you are a believer in Jesus Christ, God has promised your destination. We're going to make it! Not only has He promised our destination as the pilot of our lives, He's also promised to be in the seat next to us. We might experience turbulence in our flight of life, but God has promised our destination, He knows our journey, and He'll be there with us every step of the way.

It is clear that God is faithful. We should never again question if God is going to hold true to His promises. He will. He always will!

In closing, I want to encourage you and challenge you. If you have gone through the A-B-C's (Admit that you're a sinner, Believe that Jesus Christ is our Lord and Savior, and Commit your life to Him), then you are a Christian. You can be 100 percent confident that God will hold true to His promise of heaven for eternity. If we didn't do anything to earn our way into heaven, then how foolish are we to think that we can do anything to earn our way out of it (John 10:28). So, you don't need to get saved every week. If you meant business with God, He meant business with you.

A mother accepted Christ one Sunday morning at a church service, but the next day her son found her crying in the living room. "What's wrong?" he asked. "I don't feel like I'm saved," the mother replied. The son went into the kitchen and returned with the mother's Bible. "Well, do the verses you read yesterday still say the same things today?" the little boy asked. "Yeah, I guess so," the mother said back. "Then I guess you're still saved," said the little boy with a smile. You see, what the insightful little boy pointed out to his mother was that our salvation is based on God's promises, not emotion. So no matter how we're feeling on a particular day, God's promises still hold true.

Since God is faithful to His people and you're one of His people (if you've accepted Christ as your personal Savior), then God will be faithful to you, no matter what situations you're going through or what sins you are battling. God will never leave you.

Look for God's faithfulness in your life and write down personal examples in a journal or in your student leadership class notes so that God doesn't become simply wallpaper in your life. God is always faithful, so you can trust Him with the immediate and the eternal!

My challenge to you is to trust God with whatever you're going through right now, whether it be family issues, relationship issues, job issues, or personal struggles that you're dealing with. As one of God's children, God WILL BE FAITHFUL TO YOU!

—✕—

❷ *UNDERSTAND GOSPEL VERSES:*

John 3:3 (NIV) – *In reply Jesus declared, "I tell you the truth, no one can see the kingdom of God unless he is born again."*

—✕—

❸ *IMPROVE LEADERSHIP SKILLS:*

You can share about Jesus through your life story.

In life, your spiritual decision to follow Jesus will be challenged in every way. It will be challenged intellectually, spiritually, emotionally, etc... Others will have arguments that challenge the existence of Jesus or the validity of the Bible. No one, though, can argue against your testimony. Your experience with Jesus cannot be denied by the smartest atheist in the world!

Sharing the story of how Jesus changed your life is powerful. It is real and your friends are searching for something real. Paul was a witnessing machine. He led many people to Christ while using his testimony to share the Gospel, which is the good news that Jesus died to forgive our sins and rose again to give us life forevermore.

In Acts 26, Paul divides his story into 3 sections. Partner up with another student, open your Bibles to Acts 26:1-23, read it, and observe the following notes:

Part 1: Before Jesus changed Paul (26:1-11)
    a.   Paul was a Pharisee (26:5).
    b.   Paul put believers in jail and voted to put them to death (26:11).
    c.   Paul persecuted Christians, punished them, and tried to get them to reject/deny Jesus.
    d.   Paul sought to please man and not God (Galatians 1:10).

Part 2: Paul met Jesus (26:12-18)
    a.   Paul was on his way to Damascus (26:12).
    b.   It was about noon (26:13).
    c.   Jesus tells Paul that He will use him to be a witness to the Jews and Gentiles so that they will be exposed to the light of Christ.

Part 3: After Jesus changed Paul (26:19-23)

    a.   Paul explained that he received a vision from Jesus (26:19).

    b.   Paul's message was for everyone to repent and turn to God (26:20).

    c.   Paul was persecuted (26:21).

    d.   Paul shares about what Jesus did (26:22-23).

Now, write your testimony in three sections:

Part 1: Before Jesus Changed Me
(What was your life like before Jesus?)

Part 2: How I Met Jesus
(Consider the time, place, events in your life, and people who influenced you. This is a great place to emphasize the death, burial, and resurrection of Jesus.)

Part 3: After Jesus Changed Me
(Be sure to emphasize the joys of being a follower of Jesus, and current ways you're growing in Him.)

Now, students should partner and share Gospel-centered testimonies to each other.

Application:

Share your Gospel-centered testimony with someone this week and report back to the group how it went.

❹ LEARN LEADERSHIP PRINCIPLES:

"If you want to achieve widespread impact and lasting value, be bold."

– Howard Schultz
(Chairman and CEO of Starbucks)

—✕—

❺ DEVELOP TEAM UNITY:

Faith Fall:

Divide your students into groups of ten. Have four pairs of students face each other and lock arms across from each other, intertwined with their adjacent partner. The students should stand very close to each other and shoulder-to-shoulder. The "falling" student needs to get in line with the "catching" students and prepare to fall back-first into the arms of the "catching" students. The final student should be on the opposite side of the "falling" student for extra support and to ensure proper alignment before the fall. It is very important that an adult is supervising and making sure that each student is taking this exercise seriously as injury can occur. Once everyone is set, the exercise should use the following steps:

1. When the "falling" student is ready to fall, he/she asks out loud, "Ready?"
2. The "catching" students make sure they are ready and then say out loud, "Ready!"
3. The "falling" student then says out loud "falling."
4. The "catching" students then say out loud, "fall."
5. The "falling" student keeps his/her legs straight and falls straight back into the arms of the "catching" students.

The students rotate through until everyone has a chance to be the "falling" student.

Application:

When every student has had a chance to fall, gather the students together and reflect on the Faith Fall exercise as it relates to trust and faith. The students on a leadership team need to understand that it is very important to trust each other like family. Without trust, your team will not be effective in ministry. Also, not only do you learn to trust each other in this exercise, but you learn that just like your teammates were there to catch you, God will always be there to catch you! Faith can be a scary thing, but when you put your faith into action by trusting God and your teammates, not only are you blessed, but others will be blessed as well!

SEEK: CONNECTING WITH GOD (PART I)

❶ *BOOST BIBLICAL FOUNDATIONS:*

In the previous two sessions, we talked about trusting God
because He is faithful. In fact, we listed four ways that God
has proven Himself faithful. The question is no longer will
God hold true to His promises, but rather, will I step out and
trust His promises?

You know, it's amazing that the entire Bible can be broken
down into two main goals for a Christian to aim for every day.
The following goals are simple but essential to the Christian
life:

1. To be more like Jesus every day.
2. To tell/show others about Jesus.

Although these goals are simple and clear, it doesn't mean
that they are easy to achieve. Let's draw a graph to help us
picture what our lives look like if we are reaching our two
goals and what it looks like when we don't. Follow these
instructions:

1. Label the X axis with the number of years the average
   person lives on the earth (each mark should represent
   10 years).
2. Label the Y axis with spiritual growth marks.
3. Mark the time when you became a Christian with
   a dot (we are going to draw 3 lines that represent 3
   scenarios of what your life might look like).

4. With a purple marker, draw a line that goes diagonally up, then plateaus, and then begins to drop down. Label this line P for plateau or purple.
5. With a red marker, draw a line that looks like a roller coaster (up and down, up and down, etc.). Label this line R for rollercoaster or red.
6. For our last line, you will need a green marker. This line should be drawn as a squiggly diagonal line all the way to the same height as Jesus (as you get older, you grow closer to Jesus). Label this line G for godly or green.

Graph:

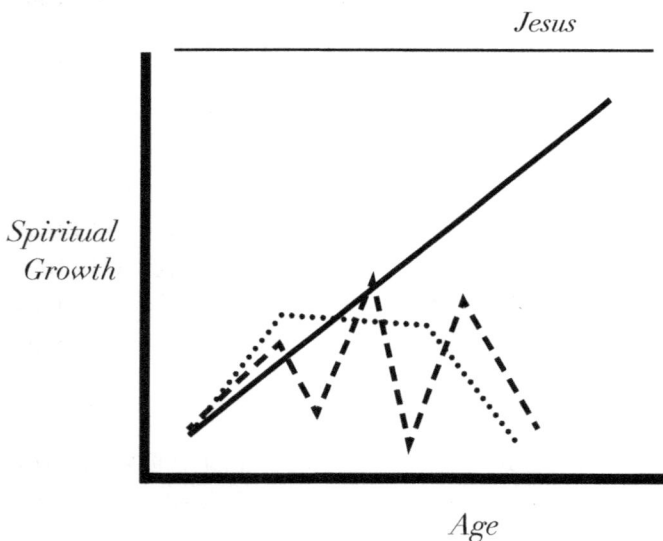

Jesus

Spiritual Growth

Age

P line: The P (plateau or purple) line represents a person who became a Christian (went through the A, B, C's...admit, believe, commit) and was very excited about the two goals of a Christian. Then something began to happen that took their excitement away. They began to just go through the motions of a Christian life. Soon, they found themselves moving away from their goal to be like Jesus.

R Line: The R (rollercoaster or red) line represents a person who became a Christian, and like the P line, was very excited about Jesus. This person soon began to move away from God for a while, but then got very excited again. This same cycle occurs through this person's entire life.

G Line: Just like the other colored lines, the G (godly or green) line committed their life to following Jesus. This person never lived a perfect life, but constantly pursued the 2 main goals of a Christian referenced earlier.

What are some things that might have caused the plateau line and the rollercoaster line to fall away from the two main goals? In other words, what are some things that might cause Christians to fall away from reaching the goal to constantly pursue after Jesus?

1. Being lonely
2. Have a bad day at school
3. Parents get divorced
4. Getting cut from the team
5. Not making the grades
6. Not going to church
7. A boyfriend or a girlfriend
8. Not spending time reading the Bible
9. Not spending time in prayer.

Should we let these circumstances cause us to fall way from God? Take time to read Psalm 42 and 43. Did you notice the chorus that was repeated 3 times?

Why are you downcast, O my soul?
Why so disturbed within me?
Put your hope in God,
For I will yet praise him,
My Savior and my God.

The Psalmist's spirits were very low as people questioned the God he served, but he did not let his emotions dictate his spiritual hunger for God. In the same way, we must not let our circumstances control our hunger for God. When things don't go our way, it hurts. It is natural for our emotions to be down, but even during the down times our heart should still pursue God. This also holds true for the good times. Many times we cannot control our circumstances, but we can control how we react to those circumstances. No matter the situation, our hearts should be in pursuit of God. If we can do this, we will find ourselves on the green line.

I know what you might be thinking: How in the world am I supposed to pursue God when my world just got flipped upside down (parents just got divorced, you just got cut from the team, etc.)? Life is a journey. There are going to be things thrown at you to get you off the path. In fact, Satan is trying to do his best to knock you off that green line (John 10:10). We want to equip you with the knowledge of how to stay on the green line no matter the circumstance.

Over the next several lessons, we are going to learn about five key words that will help you to stay on the green line. The key words are: SEEK, SUBMIT, SURROUND, SURRENDER, and STRIVE. You'll definitely want to press the record button in your mind for the next several lessons! If you can remember and apply these lessons, you will not only be able to stay on the green line, but you will be able to tell your friends how to hop on with you!

So, what is the first step to stay on the green line? The first step is to SEEK after God with everything that you are!

If I were to ask you if you would like a million dollars, what would you say? I can see you now, "Dude, a million dollars! I'd do anything to put that kind of green in my pocket..." I'm right there with you, I'd do a lot of crazy things to get those bills in my bank account. So here's what you have to do: for the next 10 days, come to this very spot and you will receive 100,000 dollars each day for a total of a million dollars.

Are you still interested?

Okay, that's not all. You can only come at 3 in the morning. You can't drive a car, ride a motorcycle, hop on a scooter, skate, or ride a bike. You can only walk or run.

Are you still interested?

Oh yeah, the weather for the next 10 days is going to be rough. The weather man said that there is a 100 percent chance of lightning, thunder, and hail.

Are you still interested?

Have you thought about all of the sleep that you are going to lose? The rules state that you can't miss school! You can't afford to miss school anyway because you have to study for your final exams that just so happen to start the day after this contest. Wow, are you still interested?

Let's take a timeout for a second. I want you to read Proverbs 2:1-6.

My son, if you accept my words and store up my commands within you, turning your ear to wisdom and applying your heart to understanding, and if you call out for insight and cry aloud for understanding, and if you look for it as for silver and search for it as for hidden treasure, then you will understand the fear of the Lord and find the knowledge of God. For the Lord gives wisdom, and from his mouth come knowledge and understanding.

Okay, the timeout is over…back to the million-dollar scenario. I'm still in, are you? I would go to great lengths for that kind of money! I would seek after that million dollars like there was no tomorrow.

Reality Check: Do you see the parallel to what God is telling us in Proverbs? When is the last time you sought after God like the million dollars? God gives us an amazing promise. He will reveal Himself to us when we seek after Him like we would a million dollars (also read Jeremiah 29:13)!

If you can make straight "A's" in the following 4 areas, there is a good chance that you are seeking after God with all that you are! Making straight "A's" will ensure that you remain on the green line.

Making Straight "A's" with God, daily.

    1. Alone (Getting one-on-one with God)

How many of you know who LeBron James is? What can you tell me about him? You can tell me a lot about him, but how many of you can say that you know LeBron James personally? You see, you've never spent time with Lebron James to truly get to know him. The same goes with God. We can learn a lot about God, but we can't truly know God unless we spend time with Him. Do you know God like you know LeBron James, or like your best friend? God wants to be your best friend, but that won't happen unless you spend one-on-one time with Him.

Jesus often spent alone time with the Father (Mt. 14:23, Mark 6:47, Luke 9:18, John 6:15, Mt. 14:13, Mark 1:35, Luke 4:42). It is very difficult to focus with so many things going on around you. If you can get alone, it will help you focus on God. The following are examples of getting alone with God.

    a. Daniel – He went upstairs in his home to pray three times a day. (Daniel 6:10).

    b. David wrote many of the Psalms while alone with God.

    c. Jesus often talked with His disciples away from the crowds (Mark 4:10, Mt. 26:20). In these alone times, He communicated great lessons to them.

Is there a right or a wrong time to get alone with God? We can have devotions at any time of the day. The key is to think about what we've read throughout the day, whether you've read them in the morning or the night before.

    a. Day and night (Psalm 1:2)

    b. At night (Psalm 63:6)

    c. All day (Psalm 119:97, Psalm 55:17)

Why should we spend one-on-one time with God? We should do so because by putting away all distractions, we leave open room and time for direct communication with God. While many youth group worship services are amazing, it's during your personal times with God that you'll see the most growth. Also, as you grow older, situations change. You might go to a different youth group or follow a different pastor, but no matter where you are, your personal time with God can stay consistent, and consistent personal time with God is essential to spiritual growth.

2. A.C.T.S (Talking with God)

Jesus spent time studying the Bible, but He also spent time in prayer. Just as Jesus did, we need to surround our Bible reading with prayer. You might be wondering, "What exactly is prayer?" Prayer is simply talking to God.

You might be asking yourself if prayer works…is it effective?

The answer is yes, prayer works and is effective. James 5:16 says that the prayer of a righteous man is powerful and effective. Some people think that prayer does not work because whatever they asked for didn't happen. We need to remember that prayer is not about God answering our wish list. It is about us having the opportunity to join in with His perfect plan. Check out 1 John 5:14-15.

When you are praying, have you ever wondered if you are really connecting with God? I mean, can He really hear us? Are my prayers just bouncing off the wall?

God promises that He does hear every word we pray to Him. Read Psalm 4:3 and Proverbs 15:29. It is an amazing thought that this BIG God, Creator of the heavens and the earth, cares enough to listen to us. We can never say that no one cares about what we think or that no one will listen to us. Every day, God cannot wait to hear from us!

We have laid out a prayer formula that is easy to follow, will help you stay focused, and will keep your perspective right as you pray. You can remember the pattern by the acronym:

A-C-T-S. Check out what each letter stands for and the prayer examples we have listed. See if you can spend a minute or two (or more) per category.

Adoration: Spend time telling God how awesome He is and why you feel this way.

Read Psalm 89:6-13

Example: Dear God, You are faithful, You are awesome, You are amazing, You are loving, You are forgiving. (To keep this section of your prayer fresh, try and work through the entire alphabet for your adoration time:
         A- God, you are awesome!
         B- God, you are big!
         C- God, you are caring! etc.)

Confession: Spend time asking God to forgive you for messing up.

Read 1 John 1:9.

Example: God, I'm truly sorry for the way I acted the other day. I have been disrespectful to my parents, I have not been listening at school, I have not been seeking after You like I should. Please forgive me. Help me to return to You and choose You daily. With Your strength, I will do better next time.

Thanksgiving: Spend time thanking God for all that He has blessed you with.

Read Phil. 4:6.

Example: God, thank You. You have blessed me with so much…my parents, my food, my house, my health, the ability to see, walk, and talk. All I have comes from You, and all that I am comes through You.

Supplication: Spend time making requests to God (remember according to His will not ours).

Read Mark 14:36. This is a good example of Jesus praying for God's will and not His will.

Example: God, I pray for my grandparents, I pray for my dad's job, and I pray that you protect our family.

Remember that while this world is filled with troubles, Christ has overcome the world (John 16:33), and while we often look to God to give us peace in certain situations, we must remember Christ Himself actually is our peace in every situation (Ephesians 2:14). After you've been through A.C.T.S., ask God to help you understand the verses that you are about to read as you begin to analyze the Bible.

Colossians 1:9-12 (NIV) - *For this reason, since the day we heard about you, we have not stopped praying for you and asking God to fill you with the knowledge of his will through all spiritual wisdom and understanding so that you may live a life worthy of the Lord and please him in every way: bearing fruit in every good work, growing in the knowledge of God, being strengthened with all power according to his glorious might so that you may have great endurance and patience, and joyfully giving thanks to the Father, who has qualified you to share in the inheritance of the saints in the kingdom of light.*

2 *UNDERSTAND GOSPEL VERSES:*

1 John 5:13 (NIV)- *I write these things to you who believe
in the name of the Son of God so that you may know that you
have eternal life.*

—✕—

3 *IMPROVE LEADERSHIP SKILLS:*

The Jesus Model of Leadership:

Cut out paper triangles and hand them out to the students.
Hold the triangle right side up (base on the bottom and
point at the top) and explain that our culture teaches that the
pyramid model is the right model of leadership. They will
tell you that the higher you move up in an organization, the
more you should be served. This model has the potential to
impact an organization temporarily.

Now, instruct the students to flip the triangle upside down
(base at the top and point at the bottom). Explain that the
inverted triangle is the Jesus model of leadership. The higher
you move up in an organization, the more you should serve
those under you. Jesus models this when he washed the
disciples' feet. Jesus tells us the first shall be last and the last
shall be first (Matthew 20:16). This model has the potential to
impact the world for eternity!

❹ LEARN LEADERSHIP PRINCIPLES:

"I don't think much of a man who is not wiser today than he was yesterday."

— Abraham Lincoln
(16th President of US, leader during the Civil War)

——✕——

❺ DEVELOP TEAM UNITY:

Hula-Hoop Pass

Circle your team of students and have them stay connected by holding hands. Have the students stay connected while passing a hula-hoop around. Once they master this task, add another hula hoop in the opposite direction. Once 2 hula-hoops are working around the circle, add another one.

Application

Ask the students how they can apply this exercise to leadership?

If the entire team doesn't focus and work together, the hula-hoop will not make it around the circle and the task will not be completed. A team needs to focus and work together to be successful.

SEEK: CONNECTING WITH GOD (PART II)

① *BOOST BIBLICAL FOUNDATIONS:*

In the last session, we studied a graph that displayed three unique lines representing a person's spiritual journey. We were challenged to make straight "A's" every day so that we could stay on the godly line (green line). We learned that it was necessary to get alone with God and away from distractions as well as praying to God while following the prayer pattern: A.C.T.S. Now, let's look at the next two words that begin with the letter "A" so that we can make straight "A's" and stay on the godly line.

3. Analyze (Listening to God through the Bible)

Just like we need physical food to survive physically, we need spiritual food to survive spiritually. Our spiritual food is the Bible, which is God's Word. If we don't get our "Jesus fill," we will spiritually starve... we will never be able to stay on the green line... we will never be ready to go to battle.

How important is the Bible to you? Several decades ago, there was a seventeen-year-old girl who lived in Asia. Check out this true story:

> *Communist soldiers had discovered the illegal Bible study. As the Pastor was reading from the Bible, men with guns suddenly broke into the home, terrorizing the believers who had gathered there to worship. The Communists shouted insults and threatened to kill the Christians. The leading officer pointed his gun at the pastor's head. "Hand me your*

Bible," he demanded. Reluctantly, the pastor handed over
his Bible, his prized possession. With a sneer on his face, the
guard threw the Word of God on the floor at his feet. He
glared at the small congregation. "We will let you go," he
growled, "but first, you must spit on this book of lies. Anyone
who refuses will be shot." The believers had no choice but to
obey the officer's order. A soldier pointed his gun at one of the
men. "You first." The man slowly got up and knelt down by
the Bible. Reluctantly, he spit on it, praying, "Father, please
forgive me." He stood up and walked to the door. The soldiers
stood back and allowed him to leave.

"Okay, you!" the soldier said, nudging a woman forward. In
tears, she could barely do what the soldier demanded. She
spit only a little, but it was enough. She too was allowed
to leave.

Quietly, a young girl came forward. Overcome with love
for her Lord, she knelt down and picked up the Bible. She
wiped off the spit with her dress. "What have they done to
Your Word? Please forgive them," she prayed. The Communist
soldier put his pistol to her head. Then he pulled the trigger.
(Jesus Freak, Volume 1, pg. 50-51)

This girl's Bible was so important to her that she gave up her
life for it! Let me ask you again, how important is your Bible
to you? Remember, for us to stay on the GREEN LINE, the
Bible needs to be important to us. As food is to our body, so
the Bible is to our soul.

Have you ever had this thought: "What if the Bible is
wrong?" Do you realize that we base our eternity on the
Bible? Forever is a long time. Eternity is so long we can't
fathom it. So, can I trust the Bible with my life and where I
will spend eternity?

The answer is yes! Look in the Bible at 2 Timothy 3:16. Fill in the blank: "All Scripture is God-_____." We will get more in depth on this subject later, but simply put, you can trust the Bible because it is God's Word. If God is perfect, then His Word must also be perfect. God has claimed and has proven to be perfect, so therefore we can trust what we read! Think back to the lesson on God's faithfulness. We talked about God being faithful to His promises and how that's seen in the Bible. Do you remember David, Peter, and the Texas illustration? If you do, you know that you can trust the Bible!

I personally feel 100 percent confident that I can trust the Bible with my eternity, but even if you don't have that much trust in God's Word, your lack of trust doesn't make it any less true. Think of it this way: I have a bridge made of toothpicks. Now, I can have 100 percent confidence that the toothpick bridge will hold me up, but when I step out onto the bridge, it will break and I will fall. On the other hand, let's say I have a bridge made of stone, firmly placed and sealed. Now I only have about 20 percent confidence that the bridge will hold me up. As I step out onto the bridge, my legs are shaking and I can hardly look down in fear of falling. Even though I doubt the stone bridge, will it still hold me up? Yes. You see, the importance isn't how much faith you have in something, it's in what or in whom you have your faith. Bottom line: God's Word is powerful and trustworthy!

You might be thinking, "Where do I start reading? The Bible is so big!" Your thinking is right. The Bible is huge. Small Bibles still have about a thousand pages. The Bible can be studied for a lifetime and still not be fully understood. At the same time, its message can be grasped by a child. I want to give you some basics on how to use this amazing book.

a. The Bible is a big book broken into two sections: The Old Testament and the New Testament. Each Testament contains smaller books. The Old Testament has 39 books and the New Testament has 27 books.
b. Each book has chapters and each chapter is broken down by verses.
c. When looking up a verse, follow this process:
   i. Go to the correct testament (look in table of contents if necessary).
   ii. Find the book.
   iii. Find the chapter.
   iv. Find the verse.

Practice: Look up Hebrews 4:12, Psalm 57:10, John 13:34,35.

How do you study the Bible?

a. Find out who wrote the book, why he wrote it, the audience of the book (who the author wrote it to), and lastly, how it applies today.
b. Make sure that the verses are consistent with the chapter, the book, the testament, and the whole Bible. If your understanding of a verse is inconsistent with another verse, then one of the verses is out of context. Your goal is to discover the meaning of the verse in the correct context. This will prevent false teaching being developed.
c. Relate what the passage meant to the audience back then to how it applies to you today.

2 Timothy 3:16-17 (NIV) - *All scripture is God-breathed and is useful for teaching, rebuking, correcting and training in righteousness, so that the man of God will be thoroughly equipped for every good work.*

Proverbs 3:1 (NIV) - *My son, do not forget my teaching, but keep my commands in your heart…*

4. Action (Living for God)

What good is a PBJ if you don't eat it…
What good are new shoes if you don't wear them…
What good is a basketball if you don't play with it…

What good is the Bible if we don't use it and do what it says…

Knowledge without action = foolishness
Knowledge with proper action = wisdom

James 1:22 (NIV) - *Do not merely listen to the word, and so deceive yourselves. Do what it says.*

Also read John 14:15, 21, 23.

Are you going to try to make straight "A's" every day? If you do, you will remain on the green line! In conclusion, earning straight "A's" with God is crucial for you to be most effective in your spiritual walk. My challenge to you today is to begin your walk with God by spending 10 minutes alone with Him each day as you work through the "A's."

———✻———

❷ UNDERSTAND GOSPEL VERSES:

John 3:16 (NIV) – *For God so loved the world that He gave His one and only Son, that whoever believes in Him shall not perish but have eternal life.*

❸ *IMPROVE LEADERSHIP SKILLS:*

Effective student leaders understand the importance of communicating vision. Will Mancini, leadership guru and author of the book, Church Unique, defines vision as "the living language that illustrates and anticipates a better future." The following notes on vision give life and practical application steps to understanding the concept of vision. These notes come directly from one of the best communicators in history, Pat Williams, who is the Vice President of the Orlando Magic:

In order to be successful in communicating your vision, the following elements must be included:

a. Believe what you communicate is important.
b. Communicate in a simple way (3 C's — Clear, Concise, Correct).
c. Communicate optimism (not enough positive in our world).
d. Communicate hope.
e. Motivation and Inspiration.
f. Great leaders do it verbally.

Application:

Jesus left us with a charge to make disciples (Matt. 28:18-20), which involves communication! Paul tells us in Romans 10:14-15 that going and telling are required for making disciples. The next time you share about Jesus to someone, apply the communication elements that you learned today and it will be a big help!

4 LEARN LEADERSHIP PRINCIPLES:

"One important key to success is self-confidence. An important key to self-confidence is preparation."

– Arthur Ashe
(Former #1 professional tennis player,
first African American to win the singles
title at Wimbledon, the US Open,
and the Australian Open)

—✗—

5 DEVELOP TEAM UNITY:

The Importance of Clarity in Communication:

Let's play the telephone game. Have all of the students get into a single file line and then have them take a seat. The leader needs to write down a three sentence statement (taken from today's lesson). The leader then needs to read these sentences in the ear of the first student in line. The first person listens and then passes on what he/she hears to the next student in line. Continue this exercise all the way to the last student. Have the last student verbalize to the entire group what he/she was told from the previous student. The leader then reads the original 3 sentences. They should be very different, unless you have the best communicators in the world in your student ministry!

Application:

Many times what we hear, process, and articulate turns out different than the original information intended. This is amplified in today's culture as we attempt to communicate quickly, exemplified when we multi-task and text using abbreviations that turn into code words. Whether you choose to communicate digitally or verbally, remember to do so in a clear, concise, and correct way.

SUBMIT: THE NEW PERSPECTIVE (PART I)

1 *BOOST BIBLICAL FOUNDATIONS:*

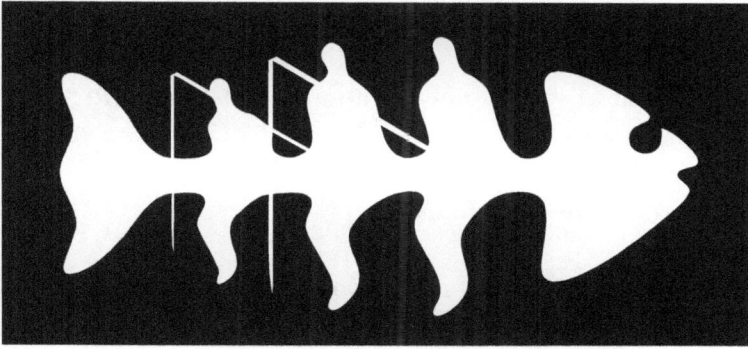

The above images are optical illusions (images not original to the authors). What do you see? It all depends on your perspective, or point of view. Perspective is defined by www. dictionary.com as "a mental view or outlook." In other words, your perspective is like a pair of glasses through which you see the world. People with different perspectives look at similar situations differently.

If you've received Jesus as your personal Lord and Savior, He's given you a new perspective and a new pair of glasses through which you can see the world as He sees it. It's left to you, then, to take off those old glasses and see the world through the new ones. I'm not making this up. Let's open up our Bibles to see what God's Word has to say about changing perspectives.

I. What change are we talking about?

A new point of view; a new creation; heart and mind set on things above.

Read 2 Corinthians 5:15-18 (NIV):

And he died for all, that those who live should no longer live for themselves but for him who died for them and was raised again. So from now on we regard no one from a worldly point of view. Though we once regarded Christ in this way, we do so no longer. Therefore, if anyone is in Christ, he is a new creation; the old has gone, the new has come! All this is from God, who reconciled us to himself through Christ and gave us the ministry of reconciliation.

Now, consider the implications and practical breakdown of this passage:

Verse 15:   Because Jesus lived a perfect life, died on the cross, and rose from the grave, He earned the right for us to STOP living for ourselves and START living for Him.

Verse 16-17:   As Christians, we should STOP looking at
               everything with worldly glasses and START
               looking at everything with Jesus glasses!

One day you might have the blessing and opportunity to
be a father or a mother. At the moment of conception, you
go from wife to mom or from husband to dad. Instead of
just one title (husband), you now have two titles (husband
and dad). Because of the birth of your child, you now have
a new title. Along with this new title, you have a different
perspective on life. Things that you used to think were
important are no longer important. You used to be selfish,
but now you care more about the baby than yourself. The
moment of conception changes your perspective forever!

In the same way, your spiritual birth (the moment you
became a Christian) changed everything. You used to live
for yourself, but at the moment you decided to follow Jesus,
you began to live for Him. You now look at the world through
your "Jesus" glasses and not your own "world" glasses.

Your perspective changes the MOMENT you become a father
or a mother. Your perspective also changes the MOMENT
you become a Christian. And as a Christian, God looks at you
in a totally different way. Read Colossians 1:21-23 (NIV):

> *Once you were alienated from God and were enemies in your
> minds because of your evil behavior. But now he has reconciled
> you by Christ's physical body through death to present you holy
> in his sight, without blemish and free from accusation— if you
> continue in your faith, established and firm, not moved from the
> hope held out in the Gospel…*

Before you were a Christian, you were alienated (separated)
from God and seen as unholy.

After you became a Christian, God is in a relationship with you and sees you as holy (we will get more into this in a later session).

It is becoming more and more clear that a Christian's perspective on life is radically different than a non-Christian's perspective. Non-Christians only have this world to look forward to. They do not realize that everything in this world is temporary. They do not realize that the only things that we will bring with us are the things that we have done that are in connection with Jesus. Christians are more motivated by what comes after this life (heaven) than temporary things during our life on earth. Paul encourages us with the same message in the book of Colossians. Check out Colossians 2:6-8 and 3:1-2 (NIV):

So then, just as you received Christ Jesus as Lord, continue to live your lives in him, rooted and built up in him, strengthened in the faith as you were taught, and overflowing with thankfulness. See to it that no one takes you captive through hollow and deceptive philosophy, which depends on human tradition and the elemental spiritual forces of this world rather than on Christ...

Since, then, you have been raised with Christ, set your hearts on things above, where Christ is seated at the right hand of God. Set your minds on things above, not on earthly things.

This is the change God has called us to, and we can accomplish it with the help of the new glasses we're supposed to put on. Before we look at what we'll see through our new glasses, let's look at why we got them in the first place.

II. Why should we (as Christians) change our perspective?

Looking again at the same four passages, you'll see clearly why our perspective should change as Christians.

2 Cor. 5:15-17:	Our perspective should change because Jesus died for us, and therefore, God reconciled us to Himself.
Col. 1:23:	We were once alienated from God and considered enemies of God, but because of Jesus' death, we are reconciled to God. Therefore, our perspective should change.
Col 2:6-8:	Let no one take you captive through hollow and deceptive philosophy, which depends on the traditions and forces of the world rather than on Christ.
Col. 3:1-2:	Jesus rose from the dead and sits at the right hand of God in heaven. Because this is a reality, we should set our hearts and minds on things above.

Alright, so what? So we've got a new pair of glasses through which we see the world—we have a new perspective. What does that mean? What's so different about how the world looks at stuff and how we should look at it? Continue on to the next lesson to find out the answers to these questions!

2 *UNDERSTAND GOSPEL VERSES:*

John 3:18 (NIV) - *Whoever believes in him is not condemned, but whoever does not believe stands condemned already because he has not believed in the name of God's one and only Son.*

—✕—

3 *IMPROVE LEADERSHIP SKILLS:*

Leaders are Learners are Readers

Ask the students to explain this phrase.

Effective student leaders are always learning. In order to learn, you must read.

Read 2 Peter 1:3-11.

Application:

Two qualities describing an effective student leader are that they are continual learners and consistent readers. If you are a leader, then you are always learning. If you are always learning, you are reading. Jay Strack, founder of Student Leadership University, is known for saying, "In five years, you'll only be a different person by the places you've been, the people you've met, and the books you've read." What books are you currently reading? What podcasts are you listening to? How are you a different person from year ago? How are you different from six months ago? How are you growing today?

4 *LEARN LEADERSHIP PRINCIPLES:*

"All successful leaders place a premium on keeping their promises and commitments."

- Steve Ventura
(Senior Professional Development Associate
for the Leadership and Learning Center)

—✂—

5 *DEVELOP TEAM UNITY:*

Listen closely to directions:

Effective student leaders listen closely to directions and then follow them.

Load up a box with as many different kinds of items like: magazines, tennis balls, paper clips, notebook paper, pens, markers, string, keys, etc. Make sure all items are visible when looking into the box.

Recruit a student to carry the box in front of the students while instructing the students to memorize what they see.

After each student has a few seconds to memorize what they see, ask the volunteer who is holding the box to exit the room.

Now, ask the team of students what kind and color were the shoes that the volunteer student was wearing.

Most of the students are confused because they thought that they were supposed to memorize the contents inside the box. But your directions were to memorize what they saw.

Part of the memorization should have been not only what they saw inside the box, but also the details of the person holding the box.

The student who pays attention to directional details will be more successful than the student who doesn't.

Application:

Listening skills are vitally important in the art of communication. Leaders must learn this skill to be effective. How many times have you skipped the directions on some homework. How did your grade turn out? Most likely, you did not receive a good grade! In life, you will receive many projects with directions attached to them as you pursue your future career. The more you listen to the directions, the more likely you will execute them correctly. The more you perform correctly, the more successful you will be! So remember to pay attention and listen!

SUBMIT: THE NEW PERSPECTIVE (PART II)...

1 *BOOST BIBLICAL FOUNDATIONS:*

In Session 5, we learned that everything changes when we take off our old glasses and put on our new glasses. We also looked at what change would take place when we submit to God's perspective as well as why the change needs to take place. Let's look at how our way of thinking changes with the new Christian perspective.

III.How exactly do I change my way of thinking?

Again, we must first recognize that the world's perspective is different. The viewpoint of the world is different than the viewpoint of God. Christians can have the same viewpoint that God does by studying His perspective. Take a look at 1 John 4:5-6 (NIV):

> *They are from the world and therefore speak from the viewpoint of the world, and the world listens to them. We are from God, and whoever knows God listens to us; but whoever is not from God does not listen to us. This is how we recognize the Spirit of truth and the spirit of falsehood.*

Now, let's look specifically at some current issues to see where the world stands as opposed to where we, as Christians, should stand.

Subject	World (1John 4:5)	Christians (1John 4:6)
Desires	- *Do whatever pleases you* - *"What happens in Vegas, stays in Vegas"*	- *Deny yourself, and take up your cross (Luke 9:23)* - *Not your will, but God's will (example: Christ, in Mark 14:35-36)*
Materials	- *Get all you can while you're here.* - *Nelson Peltz, owner of Arby's and other restaurants and businesses, purchased a 75 million dollar home in Palm Beach, Florida.*	- *Don't focus on earthly things and treasures* - *Focus on heavenly things and treasures (Matt. 6:19-21, Ph. 3:18-20)*

Motivation	- *Do it for yourself, look what I did...*	- *Do it for God (1 Cor. 10:31, Col. 3:17)*
	- *"Hate it or love it, the underdog's on top And I'm gon' shine homie until my heart stops Go ahead, envy me, I'm rap's MVP And I ain't goin' no where so you can get to know me"*	
	(50 Cent, Hate or Love It)	
Acceptance	- *Please others and self*	- *Please God (Gal. 1:10)*
	- *"And I am, whatever you say I am. If I wasn't, then why would I say I am? In the paper, the news every day I am. Radio won't even play my jam cause I am, whatever you say I am."*	
	(Eminem, The Way I Am)	

Marriage	- *Personal preference*	- *A sanctified union between a man and woman (Gen. 2:24)*
	- *A Gallup national poll taken a few years ago showed that 42% of America approves of gay marriage, which is up from 31% just a few months prior. On the flipside, 55% still oppose same-sex marriage, but that's down from 65% just a few months prior.*	
Life/ Death	- *Have fun while you can, because there's nothing after you die.*	- *To live is to exalt Christ*
	- *"Anything that feels that good couldn't possibly be bad. There's something about death that is comforting, the thought that you could die tomorrow frees you to appreciate your life now."* (Angelina Jolie)	- *To die is gain, because I'll get to spend eternity with Christ in heaven (Ph. 1:20-21)*

After we recognize that our perspectives are very different, we need to continue to change our perspective through the glasses of Jesus by renewing our mind every day. Remember from sessions 3 and 4 that if you can make straight "A's" daily, then you will be renewing your mind and keeping your Jesus glasses on. Our minds are transformed and renewed by reading the Bible and studying it. The more time we spend reading the Bible the more transformed our minds will be. The more our minds are transformed, the more we will keep our Jesus glasses on. The more we have our Jesus glasses on, the more our perspective is like Christ's. Take time to read Paul's challenge to us in Romans 12:1-2 (NIV):

> *Therefore, I urge you, brothers, in view of God's mercy, to offer your bodies as living sacrifices. holy and pleasing to God — this is your spiritual act of worship.* **Do not conform any longer to the pattern of this world, but be transformed by the renewing of your mind.** *Then you will be able to test and approve what God's will is — his good, pleasing and perfect will."*

In conclusion, we as Christians should submit to God and try to see the world as He sees it. Our challenge today is to live out Romans 12:1-2, to stop conforming to the patterns of this world, and be transformed by the renewing of our minds.

—✕—

2 UNDERSTAND GOSPEL VERSES:

Acts 16:31 (NIV) - *They replied, "Believe in the Lord Jesus, and you will be saved — you and your household."*

③ *IMPROVE LEADERSHIP SKILLS:*

Two are stronger than one:

Apply Ecclesiastes 4:12 (two are stronger than one) by working through this exercise.

Hand out the "Records Update" page from www.EquipStudentLeaders.com and give the following instructions to the students:

Explain to the students that this document was prepared to be handed out to a church congregation with the purpose of obtaining current information from everyone. This church was planning to go paperless as they would send church information via email. Challenge the students to find the mistake that is located on the front or the back of this document.

This document was prepared to capture current information, but the big problem was that the document did not ask for a current email! How would this church send out information to the congregation over the internet without having the congregations' emails!! One of the church administrators later said that they were moments away from printing thousands of these documents when another set of eyes caught the mistake. Two sets of eyes proved to be stronger than one!

Application:

Student leaders realize that two or more are stronger than one. This is a rule of thumb for almost anything in life. When working through life circumstances, two are better than one. When working for God, two are stronger than one. Don't do things alone, we are all in this together!

❹ *LEARN LEADERSHIP PRINCIPLES:*

"There is no comparison between that which is lost by not succeeding and that which is lost by not trying."
- Francis Bacon (English philosopher, statesman, scientist, and author)

—✕—

❺ *DEVELOP TEAM UNITY:*

Give every student a blank sheet of paper and instruct them to write their names on it.

Instruct the students that they will have 30 seconds to write positive attributes about the person whose name is on the sheet in front of them. After 30 seconds, the students should pass the paper to the next person and so on. When the sheet of paper arrives to its matching team member, the exercise is completed. Allow the students to read the comments written about them.

Application:

Explain to the students that an important element for a team to become closer to each other and stronger is to encourage each other. There is no room for disunity in a team that plans on being effective. This exercise will bring encouragement to every team member as well as bring the team closer together.

❶ SURROUND: LIFESTYLE OF LOVE (PART I)

BOOST BIBLICAL FOUNDATIONS:

So far we've covered God's faithfulness, seeking after God with all that we are (the four A's), and seeing the world through "God eyes." Remember, our goal as Christians is to stay on that green line and to continually grow to be more like Christ. Take a moment and look back at the graph in Session 3. This week we're looking at one of the most important topics for a Christian to not only stay on that green line, but also to show Christ to those around them.

I. The Command (Love One Another)

God tells us in the Bible that if you love Him, then you'll obey His commands (Look up John 14:15, 21, 23; John 15:9; 1 John 2:3). Alright, so the Bible is pretty clear that Christians should obey God's commands, but what is God's command?

   A. Well, to put it bluntly, we are commanded to love one another (1 John 3:11, 23; 1 John 4: 7, 11, 21).

   B. Jesus directly told his disciples this (John 13:34, 15:12, 15:17). Although the command is very simple, sometimes it is so difficult to follow. Before we look at what exactly love is, let's look at the perfect example of love: Jesus.

II. The Example (Jesus)

Jesus Christ is the ultimate example of love. He had everything, yet He paid the excruciating price for our sins by dying on a cross. Let's look at what the Bible has to tell us.

A. He first loved us (1 John 4:7, 10, 11, 19). That means that God's love for us isn't based on what we've done or what we're going to do. Even before we were Christians, God loved us (Romans 5:8). This is comforting to me because I know that God's grace and gift of heaven are based on His love (which is perfect), and not my works (which are not perfect). You can take comfort in God's love because it comes from Him first! So no matter what you've done, even if you just feel unworthy of God's love, He still loves you!

B. God is, in fact, love (1 John 4:8, 16). God is perfect. God displays the attributes of who He is, and He is the creator of everything, so it makes sense that God would not only command us to have love, but also show us His love for us. In other words, if God wasn't love and He didn't show what it meant to love, then he wouldn't be God. Just to clarify, while God is love, all love is not necessarily from God. The world tries to convince us of what it means to "love" one another or to be "in love." We must remember that when we give love that comes from God to others, we are showing Christ to those who are around us. True love comes from the One who is the Truth (John 14:6).

C. Christ showed the greatest love for us by dying for us (1 John 4:9-10; also read John 3:16; 15:13; 1 John 3:16). Probably the most quoted verse in the Bible, John 3:16, states, "For God so loved the world that he gave his one and only Son, that whoever believes in him shall not perish but have eternal life." Can you imagine giving up your son or daughter to save others? How about giving up your son or daughter for people who reject you or continually mistrust you? I don't think I could do it, but yet that's what God did. Remember, God first loved us and He is love, so even when we were considered enemies with God, He sent His Son for us. It's through Christ's payment on the cross and His resurrection that we can even go to heaven. As Christians we need to remember just how much God loves us! Jesus Christ really is the ultimate example of love.

Christ's love for us is so incredibly amazing! I find it hard to believe that He would die for me. No matter how I feel, Christ does love me and He did die for me. I'm going to heaven to spend eternity with Him someday because I believe in Christ's death, burial, and resurrection. Now that we've seen the ultimate example of love, Christ, let's look at the definition of love and what it means to actually "love one another."

—✕—

❷ UNDERSTAND GOSPEL VERSES:

Leviticus 19:2 (NIV)– *"Speak to the entire assembly of Israel and say to them: 'Be holy because I, the LORD your God, am holy.'"*

—✕—

❸ IMPROVE LEADERSHIP SKILLS:

A lot goes into pulling off a big ministry event! The following "8 P's" of Event Planning will help your team execute a successful event.

The "8 P's" of Event Planning:

1. Prayer: Pray for creative ideas, timing, details, and God
               to work through the event. When you are four
               weeks away from the event, launch a prayer
               challenge: Every day, pray for five people to
               invite to the event.

2. Purpose: Does this event align with the overall ministry
               process? The event needs to enhance your
               overall vision and goals. If it doesn't,
               continue brainstorming until you come up
               with an event that has that potential.

3. Project: What resources will we need to make the
               event a success? For example: If you are
               going to offer a hayride at your event, do you
               have access to hay, a trailer, a truck,
               and a driver?

4. Place: Where is the most effective location
               for the event?

5. Price: How much will the event cost? Is it a worthy
               investment?

6. Planning: What is the timetable for the event? Are there
               any roadblocks? What are the details? What is
               the best time of year for the event?

7. Promotion: What are the available avenues or resources
               available to promote the event? How can we
               best connect with our audience? How can
               you get the most exposure?

8. People: Who are the right people that need to be involved to make the event a success?

Continue reading for a bonus activity that will illustrate the Parable of the Talents found in Matthew 25:14-30. This will provide an opportunity to apply the "8 P's" of Event Planning while at the same time learning the lesson of investment resulting in multiplication that Jesus taught. Both leadership skills and business skills will be learned with this project.

Illustrating the Parable of the Talents:

Read Matthew 25:14-30

Give every student $5 and challenge them to invest it with the goal of at least doubling the $5 in eight weeks. Use the "8 P's" of Event Planning resource to aid in setting up a "mini business." Challenge the students that the money raised will go to a charity of the team's choice. This exercise will not only teach real life business skills and illustrate the Parable of the Talents, but it will provide money to help out the cause of your choice. There are so many options to invest and multiply the money. Allow the students to be creative and make it a point to check in with the students weekly to see how the project is going.

Make the day when the money is due a big day. Allow each student to explain how their effort went and celebrate how God used this effort to challenge, grow, and stretch the team along with impacting a cause that will change lives!

Examples of how this project can work:

1. A student can invest his/her $5 into a Lemonade stand and donate the raised money to a cause.

2. A student can invest his/her $5 into artwork and donate the raised money to a cause.

3. A student can invest his/her $5 into letters mailed out to family and friends explaining the project and the opportunity to support a cause.

4. Etc.

———✖———

❹ *LEARN LEADERSHIP PRINCIPLES:*

"Unless commitment is made, there are only promises and hopes; but no plans."

- Peter F. Drucker
(Austrian-born American management
consultant, educator, and author, whose writings
contributed to the philosophical and practical
foundations of the modern business corporation.)

———✖———

❺ *DEVELOP TEAM UNITY:*

Knock Out:

Surprise the students with a traditional game of knock out with two basketballs per line. Each line uses one basketball hoop. After you play several games, ask the students to parallel the game of knock out with spiritual leadership.

Most likely the winners had basketball shoes on, wore athletic gear, knew how to play the game, etc. Because the game of knock out was a surprise to the students, not all will be prepared to play. This presents an opportunity for a good spiritual leadership lesson.

Application:

In life, you never know what is going to come your way, just like you had no idea that we were going to play the game of knock out today. Those who wore the right shoes and right clothes were ready for the surprise game. The Bible says to always be equipped and prepared so that you're ready for spiritual victory. Effective student leaders are always spiritually prepared!

SURROUND: LIFESTYLE OF LOVE (PART II)

1 *BOOST BIBLICAL FOUNDATIONS:*

As we continue our study on surrounding ourselves with people on the godly path, we understand the command of love comes straight from God's Word and the example of love comes straight from the life of Jesus. Let's move forward and observe the definition of love and the results of living a lifestyle of love.

III. The Definition (1 Cor. 13)

1 Corinthians 13:4-8 gives a great definition for love, but before we look at the meaning of love, let's take a glance at the importance of love. Rewind three verses and check out what it's saying. The passage is speaking about different spiritual gifts, but I don't want to focus specifically on the spiritual gifts part. Notice what else 1 Corinthians 13:1-3 is saying:

> *If I speak in the tongues of men and of angels, but have not love, I am only a resounding gong or a clanging cymbal. If I have the gift of prophecy and can fathom all mysteries and all knowledge, and if I have a faith that can move mountains, but have not love, I am nothing. If I give all I possess to the poor and surrender my body to the flames, but have not love, I gain nothing.*

Do you see the pattern? Fill in the blank with whatever your spiritual gift is. Better yet, fill in the blank with whatever your talent or skill is. Also, try filling in the blank with whatever you enjoy doing.

If I _____, but I don't have love, I am nothing.

In other words, love is more important than any spiritual gift, any talent, any skill, or any hobby. Another reason why love is important is that love is what allows us to have unity within the church. We might not get along with everyone in the church, and that's fine. Some personalities get along better than others. Also, different people in the church have different abilities. With all this diversity, how then, can a church properly function? With love, that's how. Together as a church body, we are a strong force driven by God that scares the "bejeebers" out of Satan. Think of it this way... how hard is it to cut a single, solitary piece of string? Not that hard, right? Now, think of a tug of war rope, one that's really thick and strong. Can that be cut easily? No! Why is that? Are the individual strings stronger than the solitary piece? No. The reason the tug of war rope is strong is because the rope is made up of many individual strings put together. Love is the key to unity, and unity is the key to strength. Ecclesiastes 4:9-12 states the following:

> *Two are better than one, because they have a good return for their work: If one falls down, his friend can help him up. But pity the man who falls and has no one to help him up! Also, if two lie down together, they will keep warm. But how can one keep warm alone? Though one may be overpowered, two can defend themselves. A cord of three strands is not quickly broken.*

As a church body, we need to love one another, comfort those who are hurting, and encourage those who are growing. You don't have to fight spiritual battles on your own. God doesn't want you to. God will always be there for you, but hopefully, you can have good Christian friends who will be there for you too.

One last thing before we look at the meaning of love...How should we show love to others? The answer can be found in reading 1 John 3:18. It states, "Dear children, let us not love with words or tongue but with actions and in truth."

The verse explains that talk is cheap, and love is action. A husband is going to tell his wife that he loves her, right? But what does that 'I love you' mean if he mistreats treats her or doesn't help out around the house. You see, the old saying stands true: actions speak louder than words. Don't just tell your friends about Christ, but also show them Christ through loving them. Love is an action. If you tell a friend that God loves him, but then you cuss him out during a pickup basketball game, what are your actions really saying?

Alright, let's check out what the Bible says about the meaning of love in 1 Corinthians 13:4-8 (NIV):

Love is patient, love is kind. It does not envy, it does not boast, it is not proud. It is not rude, it is not self-seeking, it is not easily angered, it keeps no record of wrongs. Love does not delight in evil but rejoices with the truth. It always protects, always trusts, always hopes, always perseveres. Love never fails…

That's an amazing passage, but it's also a lot of information, so let's break it down in a chart of what exactly love is and love isn't.

Love is…	Love isn't…
patient	envious
kind	boastful
rejoicing in truth	proud
protection	self-seeking
trust	easily angered
hope	keeping record of wrongs
perseverance	rude
never failing	delighting in evil

Now that we've seen the command to love, the example of love, and the definition of love, let's look at the results of loving one another.

IV. The Results (Building Process)

Three things are going to happen if we follow God's command and love one another. As you'll see, they fit together in a building process. 1 John 4:12 states the following:

No one has ever seen God; but if we love one another, God lives in us and his love is made complete in us.

A.   First, God's love is made complete in us (1 John 4:12, 17). That means that we experience and gain a better understanding of God's love. When a man becomes a father, he gains a better understanding and a greater appreciation for his own father. In the same way, when we love one another, we gain a better understanding and appreciation of God's love for us.

B.   Second, when God's love is made complete in us, we then become more like Christ (1 John 4:12). The verse states that "God is in us." If God is in us, and we love people as Christ would love them, then we become more like Christ.

C.   Finally, when we become more like Christ, we can't help but show Christ to others (1 John 4:12; John 13:35).

The first verse states that "no one has seen God," which is true. How many of you have ever physically seen God? Neither have I. You might be the only vision of Christ that a person ever receives. Now, how many of you have ever experienced God through a kind act or comforting word by somebody else? I know I have. Christianity is more than a list of do's and don'ts It's a personal relationship with Jesus Christ that changes lives. Loving others shows people that Christianity is real and meaningful. John 13:35 states, "By this all men will know that you are my disciples, if you love one another."

The more we become like Christ, the more others will see Him. Our love for one another and for those around us is our greatest testimony for Christ. Now on the flip side, our poor behavior towards others and division amongst ourselves is our greatest hindrance to bringing people to Christ.

Conclusion: 1. Surround yourself with others that are on the green line.

2. Love others the way Jesus did and the world will take notice.

So what? What does God's command to love have to do with me, right now?

Challenge: Are you living a lifestyle of love?

1.   1 Cor. 13:4-8 (fill in the blanks with your name)

4 _____is patient, _____is kind. _____does not envy, _____does not boast, _____is not proud. 5 _____is not rude, _____is not self-seeking, _____is not easily angered, _____keeps no record of wrongs. 6 _____does not delight in evil but rejoices with the truth. 7 _____ always protects, always trusts, always hopes, always perseveres. 8 _____never fails.

2.   Do you show love to your friends, your family, even your enemies? Remember, Christ showed love to even those despised by the culture (tax collectors, prostitutes, etc.) Are you showing love to those kids who aren't exactly "cool"?

3.   Perform at least ONE loving act towards a believer and ONE towards an unbeliever each day this week.

—✕—

❷ UNDERSTAND GOSPEL VERSES:

Matthew 28:18-20 (NIV) - *Then Jesus came to them and said, "All authority in heaven and on earth has been given to me. Therefore go and make disciples of all nations, baptizing them in the name of the Father and of the Son and of the Holy Spirit, and teaching them to obey everything I have commanded you. And surely I am with you always, to the very end of the age."*

—✕—

❸ IMPROVE LEADERSHIP SKILLS:

Refer to the Row Boat Handout in the Resources section of www.EquipStudentLeaders.com. Draw the three boats on the board and interact with the students as you work through the scenarios.

Application:

Many times, Satan tries to disrupt God's work by setting up scenarios similar to Boat A. Make sure you make every effort to paddle on Boat C. A unified team moving in the same direction with a common goal cannot be stopped! Once a team allows for even the slightest of disunity to creep in, effectiveness decreases. Be certain that your team maintains unity at all times. When disunity occurs, quickly and correctly deal with it before separation occurs.

—✕—

④ *LEARN LEADERSHIP PRINCIPLES:*

"To tend unfailingly, unflinchingly, towards a goal, is the secret of success."
- Anna Pavlova
(a Russian ballerina of the late 19th and 20th century. Widely regarded as one of the finest classical ballet dancers in history.)

—✕—

⑤ *DEVELOP TEAM UNITY:*

Two Truths and a Lie:

This is another good exercise for a student group to get to know each other better. Move around the room and have each student verbalize two truths and one lie about themselves. Have the other students try and guess which statements are factual and which one is false.

Application

It is important to know your team members. It is also fun to learn some surprising facts about them! Throughout the year, continue to dialogue with your teammates and learn new facts. You'll find that your leadership team will become like a family.

SURRENDER: THE NEW ATTITUDE (PART I)

1 *BOOST BIBLICAL FOUNDATIONS:*

In Sessions 7 and 8, we talked about God's love and how
we as Christians should surround others with that love. In
this lesson, we're going to talk about how we can stay on the
green line when things are going great, or when things get
tough. When it comes down to it, how you react in situations
can be summarized in one word: attitude. Now, when I
searched the scriptures for "attitude," I found that there are
two main battles that take place that decide what kind of
attitude I'm going to have in a given situation. Those two
battles are pride vs. humility and happiness vs. joy.

I.   When Life is Great!!!

Pride	*vs.*	*Humility*
- Look what I've done (Ph. 3:4-8)		- Look what God's done
- Takes credit for everything		- Gives God the credit for everything (1 Cor. 10:31)
- Approval dependent		- Not approval dependent (Ph. 2:5-8)
Happiness	*vs.*	*Joy*
- Based on circumstances		- Not based on circumstances (Ps. 32:11)
- Based on self		- Not based on self (Ph. 4:4)
- Continual search for pleasure		- Continual search for God

Illustrations and explanations for when life is great:

Pride: Paul writes in Philippians 3:4-8 that if anyone has
            anything to be prideful about, he's got more.
            He was circumcised, a Jew, an expert in the law,
            and with regards to legalism (focus on do's and
            don'ts and strict rules of religion), he was
            faultless. So did Paul brag? No. He says in verse
            eight that those things are all rubbish compared
            to Christ.

            - Some pro athletes are the perfect example of
            people with bad attitudes. How many players do
            you know of that beat their chest, pop their jersey,
            or demand more money every time they score a
            point? Everything points back to self.

            - Think back to the perspective lesson. Remember
            all those quotes from celebrities. They were all
            self-driven and approval dependent. What can I
            do to better my situation and get people to like
            me?

Humility: Thinking back to the perspective lesson,
            remember that looking through "God eyes" we
            don't need to live for the approval of others. On
            the contrary, we should be living to please God,
            and living to help others.

            - Who is the ultimate example of humility? Once
            again, we must look at the life of Jesus (Are you
            starting to sense a pattern in these lessons...that
            everything points back to Jesus?). Philippians 2:5-
            8 (NIV) states the following:

Your attitude should be the same as that of
Christ Jesus: Who, being in very nature God,
did not consider equality with God something
to be grasped, but made himself nothing, taking
the very nature of a servant, being made in
human likeness. And being found in
appear ance as a man, he humbled himself
and became obedient to death–even
death on a cross!

Talk about having it all! Jesus was God, He had everything. Yet He loved us so much (look back to Session 4) that He humbled himself. When He had it all, He became a servant and died on a cross for us.

- How does humility play out for you? When things are going well, give credit to God, and turn the focus. If your focus is other people, then you won't get "blindsided" when things get tough.

Happiness: C.S. Lewis writes that as humans, it's not that we don't pursue joy too strongly, but rather "we are far too easily pleased."

- Think of it this way. Picture a restaurant that has all your favorite foods: steak, shrimp, pasta, ice cream, chocolate covered whatever you want, etc. Now picture that it's all-you-can-eat, and your ticket's been paid for. You walk right up to the door, and turn left to go around the side of the building. You head straight to the dumpster and dive right in... Banana peels, leftover liver, dirty baby diapers... You're probably thinking, some one would be crazy to pass up that feast. It's right next door. You know what? You're right, but yet that's what we do all the time. We pass up the feast of knowing our Creator and Savior and seeing what He has in store for us. Instead we choose the dumpster filled with junk like self-absorption, alcohol, drugs, sex, and popularity.

- If you're pursuing happiness instead of true joy that comes from God, then you're never going to be satisfied. Why is it that superstars and rock stars are some of the people who use drugs the most? It's because they have everything yet are not satisfied. They continue to search for the next pleasure in worldly things. I'm sorry to break this to you, but if you've been searching for satisfaction from places other than God, you're not going to be fulfilled. Sooner or later, you're going to feel empty.

Joy: While it's perfectly fine to be excited by getting a new bike, getting a good grade on a test, or making the last-second shot, it's important to understand the difference here. If you have true joy, then yes, you're going to be excited and happy when good things happen to you, but that doesn't become the foundation of who you are. You understand the greater good and joy.

- We're actually commanded to have joy (Psalm 32:11, Philippians 4:4). Too often people confuse Christianity with the idea of emotionless obedience to a list of do's and don'ts. We were created by a personal God who sent His Son to die for us. On top of that, to be obedient to Him actually means to be joyful. Christianity isn't meant to be a bore. We were created by an all-powerful God who wants to have a personal relationship with us, and He promises to be there for us at all times (look back at the Foundation of Faithfulness lesson). Christianity should be the most intense, exciting, and joyful experience anybody could ever know! All we have to do is seek God, and trust Him for the outcome!

- Our joy should be in God and based on serving the needs of others. Think of it this way: if a husband were to bring home a bouquet of flowers for his wife and said, "Honey, I brought you some flowers so that you'll cook me a meal," what do you think she would say? She'd be upset, wouldn't she? Wouldn't you? The husband should say something like, "Honey, I brought you flowers because I love you." Good deeds should be selfless, not selfish in nature. Doing something solely for God and the joy of helping others takes the focus off yourself. When you take the focus off yourself, then pride is taken out of the picture. John Piper once stated, "God is most satisfied in us when we are most satisfied in Him."

—✕—

❷ *UNDERSTAND GOSPEL VERSES:*

Luke 9:23 - *Then he said to them all: "If anyone would come after me, he must deny himself and take up his cross daily and follow me."*

❸ IMPROVE LEADERSHIP SKILLS:

Pat Williams is the Vice President of the Orlando Magic.
Pat is respected in all walks of life as he has been involved
with major leadership positions and written many books.
In one of his lectures on leadership, he has expressed the
importance of character within a leader. Leaders understand
that character counts! Williams gave the following qualities
that make up great character:

1. Honesty: Make it a goal to tell the truth in all situations.
2. Integrity: Who you are when no one is looking matters.
3. Consistency: Keeping on keeping on will earn trust.
4. Responsibility: Owning your duties is mature.
5. Humility: Servant leadership is the biblical
   model of leadership.

Application:

General Schwarzkopf once said: "Leadership requires
strategy and character. If you have to do without one, make it
strategy." Every day, build your character. Remember it takes
a long time but it can be ruined quickly.

—✕—

❹ LEARN LEADERSHIP PRINCIPLES:

*"Knowledge is power and knowledge shared is power
multiplied."*

- Bob Noyce
(Cofounder of Fairchild Semiconductor
in 1957 and Intel Corporation in 1968)

⑤ *DEVELOP TEAM UNITY:*

Untangled:

Circle the students in teams of 8-10 and instruct them to grab the arms across from them. Once everyone is connected, tell the students that their goal is to work together to untangle themselves. The first group to untangle is the winner!

Application:

Ask the students how they can apply this exercise to leadership. For a team to be successful, it takes teamwork, focus, concentration, and patience!

SURRENDER: THE NEW ATTITUDE (PART II)

❶ *BOOST BIBLICAL FOUNDATIONS:*

Reviewing Session 9, we looked at maintaining a humble and joyful spirit when life is going well. This seems like it would be easy to do, but it's not because our pride gets in the way. Let's look at our attitudes in relation to when life goes bad.

II.   When Life Gets Rough!!!

Pride	*vs.*	*Humility*
- Look what I've suffered		- Look at God's faithfulness (2 Cor. 6:3-10)
- Seeks personal understanding		- Trusts God for the outcome (Ph. 2:9-11)
- Blames others		- Takes responsibility

Happiness	*vs*	*Joy*
- Impossible to be happy		- True joy found in Christ (Ph 1:21)
- Look for substitutes		- Look to share with others

Illustrations and Explanations for when life gets rough:

Pride: - You might not think that pride would be an is
           sue when it comes to suffering, but actually it's
           just as prevalent in bad times as it is in good

times. It only takes a different form. John Piper states that while pride in good times says, "Look what I've done," pride in bad times says, "Look what I've suffered." Do you see the similarity? How many of your friends always complain about what they're going through, even when it seems to be the smallest of inconveniences? How many times have you found yourself complaining over the small stuff?

- Now, just as Paul had the most to brag about in Ph. 3:4-8, he also had the most to complain about in 2 Cor. 6:3-10. Paul needed endurance, he was in trouble, suffered hardships, was beaten, imprisoned several times, caught in riots, forced to work extremely hard, had many sleep less nights, starved at times, disliked, considered dying, and had nothing. Through all of this, he still was able to have a godly attitude and trust that God would bring him through those trials.

- It's human nature to seek understanding for why bad things happen. Unfortunately, we don't always grasp why things happen. It's easy to take in news of something bad happening to a bad person. But what about when something bad happens to a good person? That's a little tougher to swallow. I still struggle with that one, but eventually, I always come back to the idea that God is bigger than whatever I'm going through, and He's got a plan for me that I might not know about. Even though we might not understand God on our terms, we have to remember that we serve a faithful God (refer back to Session 1), and we can trust God. God never promised us an easy road, but He did promise us the destination and safe passage through to the other side.

- Lastly, when things are great, we want the credit, but when things go bad, it's always some body else's fault. Again, look at pro athletes. When a team starts to lose, players blame the coach, the coach blames the management, and the management fires either the players or the coach, depending on whose fault they think it is.

Humility: If you find yourself doubting God's faithfulness, think back to the Texas/quarter illustration from Session 1. We don't serve a God of chance. I know situations get tough, and I know we don't always understand them, but that's when we have to humble ourselves the most and say, "God, I'm giving it up to You."

- A humble person trusts God for the outcome. For an example we turn to Christ. Check out Philippians 2:9-11 (NIV):

> *Therefore God exalted him to the highest place and gave him the name that is above every name, that at the name of Jesus every knee should bow, in heaven and on earth and under the earth, and every tongue confess that Jesus Christ is Lord, to the glory of God the Father (emphasis added).*

Jesus trusted God for the outcome, and in the end, God exalted Him to the highest place. Do you think it was fun and easy for Jesus to go through the pain of dying on a cross? Absolutely not! Yet, He loved us so much and trusted God that He did it anyway.

- Also, when something bad has happened, and you know that it's your fault, show humility and take responsibility for your actions. I found through experiences growing up, that whenever I denied things and blamed other people, the pun ishment was worse and more people ended up hurt than if I had just told the truth the first time.

- We're humans, and we're going to mess up. It's not a matter of messing up, but rather admitting your mistakes and learning from them. People will respect you more if you're upfront, humble, and honest.

Happiness: Think back to all that Paul suffered. When he wrote to the Philippians, he was in prison. Do you think Paul was happy about his circumstances? Do you think it would be possible to be happy in those circumstances? No, but the real question is, did Paul base his attitude on his circumstances? NO WAY! I know that to be true because despite what Paul was going through, he used the term "joy" (in some shape or form) 18 times in his small (four chapter) letter to the Philippians!

- You see, when a person searches for happiness and meaning in things other than God, he or she ends up empty inside. In order to fight the emptiness, he or she searches for substitutes in the way of idols like drugs, alcohol, materials, sex, etc.

Joy: Remember, true joy is found in Christ. Paul
          writes in Phil. 1:21 that "to live is Christ" and "to
          die is gain." That means that life, with all its ups
          and downs, is meant to glorify Christ. Christ is
          constant and His promises are true so you can
          praise God during the bad times just as much
          as you can during the good times. One of the
          biggest fears of unbelievers is death because
          death brings the end. On the contrary, if you're
          a Christian, death is the beginning. It's the be
          ginning of an eternity spent with God in heaven!
          So if life's greatest defeat is our greatest triumph,
          what can this world bring at us that we
          can't handle?

In conclusion, we as Christians must surrender ourselves
to God and commit to having a humble and joyful attitude,
no matter the circumstance!! As your challenge this week,
ask yourself this question: Whatever situations that arise
this week, am I going to stay on the green line by being
humble and joyful?

This week, I want you to give yourself a five second attitude
check every hour on the half-hour. Now, I understand that
you're not going to be near a clock 24 hours a day and that
you're not going to remember to check the clock every hour.
The goal of this assignment is to help you get in the habit
of checking your attitude. Let's say you look up at the clock
and it's around 3:30. Briefly, think through in your head if
you're having a humble and joyful attitude. The more you
can meditate on God's Word and what it says, the better the
attitude you're going to have, no matter the situation!

2 *UNDERSTAND GOSPEL VERSES:*

1 John 1:9 - *If we confess our sins, he is faithful and just and will forgive us our sins and purify us from all unrighteousness.*

———✕———

3 *IMPROVE LEADERSHIP SKILLS:*

Work Smart:

Pass the "Numbers" worksheet (located on www.EquipStudentLeaders.com) out to students face down. Challenge the students to circle the numbers in numerical order until all of the numbers are circled. The first to finish and explain their method of locating all of the numbers quickly wins!

Application:

Working hard is honorable, but not as effective as working smart. For example, Student A and Student B both did their best in their attempt to complete this exercise. Student A did his/her best on this exercise, but never figured out the pattern in which the numbers were laid and therefore finished after Student B. Why did Student B finish faster? Student B was able to figure out the pattern that the numbers were laid out in which made it easier and quicker to complete the task. Student B was able to figure out that the numbers were displayed in four quadrants in numerical order, moving in a clockwise direction. If you fold the paper into four quadrants, it even makes this assignment easier. Demonstrate this method to all of the students.

Challenge the students that this exercise can be applied in real life situations. The students who do their best along with reading the instructions and thinking about the best possible way to accomplish a task will be more effective than the students who just work hard without thinking first.

—✕—

4 *LEARN LEADERSHIP PRINCIPLES:*

"It's not whether you get knocked down, it's whether you get up."

-Vince Lombardi
(Head Coach for the Green Bay Packers,
led the team to 5 championships in just 7 years)

—✕—

5 *DEVELOP TEAM UNITY:*

Obstacle course:

Prior to the lesson, use a room or rooms to set up an obstacle course by using chairs, mobile dividers, etc.

Separate your students into groups of five and tell them that each team member will have a unique role in this exercise.

Team Member 1:   - will be blindfolded with the goal of being guided through the obstacle course by other team members. It is important to note that this person needs to only listen to the voices that he/she trusts because some team members will be assigned to relay bad directions.

Team Member 2: Provide the blindfolded team member with the correct information to guide (only with voice) him/her to the finish line without bumping into anything.

Team Members
3, 4, & 5: Provide the blindfolded team member with incorrect information that will cause him/her to have a difficult time hearing the correct information.

Application:

When all teams are finished, ask students how they can apply the exercise to leadership. In our world, people giving false directions are loud, and there are many who try to provide incorrect directions. It is very important to listen closely and discern the good from the bad. If you can do this, you will avoid many obstacles and reach your goal successfully!

STRIVE: THE NEW STANDARD (PART I)

1 *BOOST BIBLICAL FOUNDATIONS:*

So far, we've learned that if we want to be an effective
Christian, then we must remain on the green line (remember
Session 3). We have equipped you to do so by learning and
applying the "S" words: SEEK, SUBMIT, SURROUND,
SURRENDER, and STRIVE. We have learned that if
these action words are the centerpiece of our lives, than
we will remain on the green line, and therefore make a big
impact for God.

The word of the day is STRIVE. The green line standard of
living for a Christian is dramatically different than that of
the non-Christian. What standard do non-Christians set for
themselves? Maybe their parents give them boundaries to
follow, maybe they picked up on certain rules during school,
or maybe they have developed their own standard to live by.
Is there a right and wrong standard of rules to follow? Can
we just live for ourselves, not bother anyone, and be okay?
Does the way we live our lives impact others?

A while back, Pink was asked if she cared about her
position as a role model by Launch magazine. Check out
Pink's response:

> **LAUNCH:** So you were pretty rebellious. I'm sure if you
> could do it all over again, you wouldn't change a thing,
> but do you ever worry about the example you set as a role
> model for your fans?

Pink: I always knew when to draw the line. I always had that inner voice that told me what was right and what was a little too much.

My question for Pink is, "What was the inner voice that set her standard of living?" If everyone has an inner voice that tells them what is right or wrong, then does that inner voice set the same standard of right and wrong for everyone? The truth is that many people have standards, but they are not the standards that the Bible has set. Pink has set a standard of living for herself, but does it match up with the standard that the Bible has set?

Our culture is doing their best to live for themselves, but also feel good about themselves spiritually. In other words, many times, they take what the Bible says and then twist it to say things that they want it to say. No one wants to feel bad about themselves. No one desires to change the way that they are living their lives. What a deal… you can feel like you are pleasing God, while at the same time you can live the life that you want to live. Check out what Justin Timberlake said in an edition of Rolling Stone magazine:

> ….*as a kid, he (Justin) attended a nearby Baptist church with his folks but felt rejected by its frowning, judging elders and eventually found his own place with the Lord, no church required. "I can honestly say I am a Christian, but my spirituality has been developed on the road and is based on my experiences with God" (Rolling Stone, January 23, 2003).*

There is a huge problem with the above examples! Pink thinks that the standard that her inner voice tells her to have is good enough for her role model status. Justin feels like he can call himself a Christian, but at the same time live the way that he desires to live. Both of these examples are far from what the Bible says. In fact, they are in different galaxies! The Bible says that we should strive everyday to live like Jesus did. This means that we STOP living the way that pleases the self and we START living for Jesus. Check out Luke 9:23 (NIV):

> *Then he [Jesus] said to them all, "If anyone would come after me, he must deny himself and take up his cross daily and follow me."*

WOW! The bar is raised very high! Jesus requires us to totally deny what we want and instead receive what He wants for our lives. This isn't a bad thing. Yes, life is not always going to be easy, but the more we act in obedience to Jesus, the more true freedom we find (John 8:31-32). Let's take a look at examples of the type of standard that we are striving to reach. We are going to cover five major areas that make up God's standard of living for our lives.

1. The Standard: A Call to Perfection

First, we are going to look at some verses that clearly spell out the actions of a Christian.

Romans 13:12-14
"...let us put aside the deeds of darkness and put on the armor of light...let us behave decently, as in the daytime, not in orgies and drunkenness, not in sexual immorality and debauchery, not in dissension and jealousy. Rather clothe yourselves with the Lord Jesus Christ, and do not think about how to gratify the desires of the sinful nature."

Ephesians 5:1-10
"Be imitators of God...live a life of love...among you there must not be even a hint of sexual immorality, or of any kind

of impurity, or of greed, because these are improper for God's holy people....nor... obscenity, foolish talk or coarse joking... because of such things, God's wrath comes on those who are disobedient. Therefore do not be partners with them...you were once darkness, but now you are light in the Lord. Live as children of light..."

1 Corinthians 6:19-20
"Do you not know that your body is a temple of the Holy Spirit, who is in you, whom you have received from God? You are not your own; you were bought at a price. Therefore honor God with your body."

1 Peter 1:15, 16
"But just as he who called you is holy, so be holy in all you do... be holy, because I am holy."

1 Thessalonians 4:3-8
"It is God's will that you should be sanctified: that you should avoid sexual immorality; that each of you should learn to control his own body in a way that is holy and honorable, not in passionate lust like the heathen, who do not know God...for God did not call us to be impure, but to live a holy life...he who rejects this instruction does not reject man but God..."

Matthew 5:48
"Be perfect, therefore, as your heavenly Father is perfect"

Jesus says that we should strive for perfection in our actions, but it's not only about actions. It's also about our thoughts. I've met some people that think they can think anything they want as long as they don't put feet to the action. In other words, they feel that as long as their actions are okay with God, then their thought life can be whatever they want it to be. For example, some married guys think that it's okay to think about other girls as long as they don't do anything with these girls. They think it's alright to look at the menu as long as they don't place an order. But, the Bible says that it's not just about our actions, it's also about our thoughts.

Second, let's take a look at the Bible verses that reinforce the truth of making every thought pleasing to God.

Job 31:1
"I won't "look lustfully at a girl."

Matthew 5:28
"But I tell you that anyone who looks at a woman lustfully has already committed adultery with her in his heart."

2 Corinthians 10:5
"…we take captive every thought to make it obedient to Christ."

Philippians 4:8
"Whatever is true… noble… right… pure… lovely… admirable… think about such things."

It's not only about our actions and our thoughts behind our actions, but it's also about our motivation behind both our thoughts and our actions. For example, I could help an old lady cross the street. Now, my motive could be to honor God, or it could be that I'm hoping that she will give me a Little Debbie Snack Cake as a reward for helping her! Although it is a very nice thing to help an old lady across the street, God doesn't give me credit for the action if I do it for my own personal gain. He will give me credit if I am doing the action to bring Him Glory… if I do it to make Him smile. God requires our actions, our thoughts, and our motives to be pure.

Third, let's check out the following verses that support the truth of keeping our motives pure before God.

Psalm 19:14
"May the words of my mouth and the meditation of my heart be pleasing in your sight..."

Psalm 104:34
"May my meditation be pleasing to him, as I rejoice in the Lord."

1 Corinthians 4:5
"Therefore judge nothing before the appointed time; wait till the Lord comes. He will bring to light what is hidden in darkness and will expose the motives of men's hearts. At that time each will receive his praise from God."

1 Corinthians 9:24
"Do you not know that in a race all the runners run, but only one gets the prize? Run in such a way as to get the prize."

Ephesians 5:3,4
"But among you there must not be even a hint of sexual immorality, or of any kind of impurity, or of greed, because these are improper for God's holy people. Nor should there be obscenity, foolish talk or coarse joking, which are out of place, but rather thanksgiving."

Maybe before going through a spiritual boot camp like Equip, you thought it was okay to entertain thoughts that are not pleasing to God. Or maybe you thought it was cool to do good things even though your motivation was for yourself. Maybe you've never been challenged with striving for such a high standard. Okay, so it is clear that my actions, thoughts, and motives need to be pleasing to God. The Bible, though, even raises the bar higher. It says that we need to avoid the environments that promote things that are not pleasing to God. We need to stay away from evil!

Fourth, take a look at the verses that support the truth of staying away from environments that are not pleasing to God

1 Thessalonians 5:22
"Avoid every kind of evil."

Psalm 101:2-4
"I will be careful to lead a blameless life…I will walk in my house with a blameless heart…I will set before my eyes no vile thing…men of perverse heart shall be far from me…I will have nothing to do with evil."

2 Corinthians 6:14-18
"Do not be yoked together with unbelievers. For what do righteousness and wickedness have in common? Or what fellowship can light have with darkness? What agreement is there between the temple of God and idles? For we are the temple of the living God…Therefore come out… and be separate… touch no unclean thing and I will receive you…"

Psalm 1:1
"Blessed is the man who does not walk in the counsel of the wicked or stand in the way of sinners or sit in the seat of mockers."

Believe it or not, we are going to take it a step further. The Bible not only says that we need to AVOID evil or sinful environments, but that we need to come to the point where we HATE things that are not pleasing to God and environments that are full of sin. Some reach a point where they are so entangled by sin that they end up enjoying sin. Or maybe they don't actually enjoy the sin, but they definitely don't HATE it! I've been at this point. Have you? The Bible says that we should have the desire to avoid evil. We must get to a point to where we feel the same about sin that God does. The more that we align ourselves with God, the more we will see sin as He sees it. In other words, the longer that we are on the GREEN line, the more we will HATE the things that are not of God.

Fifth, read the verses that reinforce the truth of hating evil.

Psalm 97:10
"Let those who love the Lord hate evil, for he guards the lives of his faithful ones and delivers them from the hand of the wicked."

Romans 12:9
"Love must be sincere. Hate what is evil; cling to what is good."

Psalm 5:4
"You are not a God who takes pleasure in evil; with you the wicked cannot dwell."

Psalm 34:14
"...turn from evil and do good..."

Proverbs 15:26
"The Lord detests the thoughts of the wicked, but those of the pure are pleasing to him."

Proverbs 8:13
"To fear the Lord is to hate evil; I hate pride and arrogance, evil behavior and perverse speech."

II. The Battle: Sin Nature vs. Spirit Nature

The standard described by the above five areas seems impossible to reach! It seems like God is demanding a lot from us, doesn't it? How in the world are we supposed to keep His standard? The bar has been set way too high! Maybe you feel like one of the following scenarios:

* I feel like I'm swimming upstream, but the current is too strong to fight. I'm ready to give up and start flowing with the current that is heading down stream.

* I feel like I'm being asked to dunk a basketball on a 20 foot rim... without legs!

* I feel like I'm being asked to live a boring life. God does not want me have any fun!

It is normal to be thinking these things. God is asking us to do something that is impossible to do on our own. Because of this, we are going to struggle between letting God have control and keeping control for ourselves. In the book of Romans, Paul also finds himself struggling with the standard that God has given us in Romans 7:14-25 (NIV).

(vs. 19-20) *"...for what I do is not the good I want to do; no the evil I do not want to do, this I keep on doing...now if I do what I do not want to do, it is no longer I who do it, but it is sin living in me that does it..."*
(vs. 21-23) *"...So I find this law at work: when I want to do good, evil is right there with me. For in my inner being I delight in God's law; but I see another law at work in the members of my body, waging war against the law of my mind and making me a prisoner of the law of sin at work within my members..."*

(vs. 24-25) *"...Jesus will rescue us from our body of death...
so then, I myself in my mind am a slave to God's law, but in the
sinful nature a slave to the law of sin..."*

Because it is normal to struggle with God's standard, have
you ever had this thought run through your mind: "I know
God doesn't what me to _____ (fill in the blank),
so I'm going to _____ (fill in the blank) and ask for
forgiveness after." For example: "I know God doesn't want
me to steal the Twinkie box from the store, so I'm going to
steal it and ask God to forgive me." God is a God that is full
of grace and forgiveness, but He doesn't give this to us when
we try to take advantage of Him.

Romans 6:1, 2
*"... shall we go on sinning so that grace may increase? By no
means! We died to sin, how can we live in it any longer?"*

Galatians 5:13
"...do not use your freedom to indulge in the sinful nature..."

1 Peter 2:16
*"...live as free men but do not use your freedom as a cover up
for evil..."*

Think about some of the struggles that you have right now
in your spiritual journey. Have you ever thought that there
is no way that you could overcome them? And because you
conclude that you cannot overcome it, you just accept that
you will submit to that temptation and sin for the rest of your
life. We need to realize that if we cannot get past certain sins,
that we are controlled by that sin. For example, if I commit
to not watch TV for an entire day, but I can never fulfill this
commitment...then, the TV has some control in my life. It is
the same with sin. If I cannot give it up, then it has control

of me. If I am controlled by anything other than God, I cannot please God.

Romans 8:8
"...those controlled by the sinful nature cannot please God..."

Why do we struggle with the desire to do things that do not meet God's standard? What is the battle that is going on inside of us? The Bible says in Galatians that the BATTLE is sinful nature vs. the Spirit.

Galatians 5:17
"...for the sinful nature desires what is contrary to the Spirit and the Spirit what is contrary to the sinful nature. They are in conflict with each other..."

Our old sin nature (1 John 2:15-17, Gal. 5:19-21)
Our new Spirit nature (Galatians 5:22-25)

———✕———

❷ *UNDERSTAND GOSPEL VERSES:*

John 14:6 - *Jesus answered, "I am the way and the truth and the life. No one comes to the Father except through me."*

———✕———

❸ *IMPROVE LEADERSHIP SKILLS:*

Decision Grid:

Throughout our entire life, we will regularly come to intersections where we are forced to choose between two or more options. What do we choose? How do we choose? The following decision grid will lead to Godly wisdom at our life's intersections. Ask yourself the following questions:

1. Is the Bible clearly okay with this decision?
(John 8:31)

2. Are you obeying the rules / law with this decision?
(1 Peter 2:13-14)

3. Are your parents okay with this decision?
(Ephesians 6:1)

4. Will this decision encourage your walk with God?
(Ephesians 5:1)

5. Will this decision help your Christian witness with others?
(1 Cor. 10:24, 32)

If the answer is yes to the above questions, you will be making a decision with godly wisdom!

—✕—

❹ *LEARN LEADERSHIP PRINCIPLES:*

"If the family were a boat, it would be a canoe that makes no progress unless everyone paddles."
-Letty Cottin Pogrebin
(Writer, Feminist Advocate, One of founding editors of Ms. Magazine, Co-founder of the National Women's Political Caucus, Political activist on topics such as hunger and Israeli-Palestinian conflict)

5 DEVELOP TEAM UNITY:

Mix up shoe relay:

Divide students into two teams. Line them up into two lines. Line 1 takes off their shoes and piles them up 20 yards in front of Line two. Line two takes off their shoes and piles them up 20 yards in front of Line one. The students in the front of the line each run to the pile of shoes that is in front of them, puts a pair of shoes on of their choice and then runs back to their line. Each line does this until everyone has participated. The line that finishes first, wins!

Application:

Ask students how you can apply this relay to spiritual leadership. It is not easy to put someone else's shoes on because they might not fit your feet. Even though it is not easy, it is necessary if you are going to be effective at the relay game. In life, sometimes it's not easy connecting with others. God calls us to connect with others and to do so effectively. You must get into their shoes!

STRIVE: THE NEW STANDARD (PART II)...

❶ *BOOST BIBLICAL FOUNDATIONS:*

Now that we have established the standard that God calls us
to live by as well as the battle between the sin nature and the
Spirit nature, it's time to reveal the strategy for victory. Satan
appears to be winning this battle of purity, so we must fight
harder! Continue to work through this last session and make
sure to win this battle that so many are losing.

III. The Strategy: How to Win the Battle
Can I have victory over sin, or should I accept sin
mastering me?

Romans 6:14
*"...for sin shall not be your master, because you are not under
law, but under grace..."*

Romans 6:8-11
*"...Christ died on the cross...Christ rose again....we died with
Christ...we rose with Him...since Christ beat death, death no
longer has mastery over him. The death he died, he died to sin
once for all, but the life he lives, he lives to God. In the same way,
count yourselves dead to sin but alive to God in Christ Jesus."*

1 Corinthians 6:12
*"...everything is permissible for me but not everything is
beneficial...but I will not be mastered by anything..."*

Galatians 5:24

"Those who belong to Christ have crucified the sinful nature with its passions and desires."
Ephesians 1:19-20
"May our hearts be enlightened that we may know the "incomparably great power" given "for us who believe. That power is like the working of his mighty strength, which he exerted in Christ when he raised him from the dead and seated him at his right hand in the heavenly realms..."

Who set us free from the law of sin and death? Jesus has set us free with His death, burial, and resurrection. I need to identify God's role in this and embrace His grace.

Romans 8: 1-4
(vs. 1- 2) *"Therefore, there is now no condemnation for those who are in Christ Jesus, because through Christ Jesus the law of the Spirit of life set me free from the law of sin and death."*

Colossians 1:21-23
God sees us through Christ: holy and blameless, "free from accusation..."

1 John 1:7
"...and the blood of Jesus, His Son, purifies us from all sin."

Why do I sometimes desire the sinful nature (the things of the world) and sometimes desire the Spirit (the things of God)? The Bible spells out clearly that we will desire whatever we fill our minds with. If I am filling my mind with the things that are of the world, then I will desire the things of the world. If I am filling my day with TV that is not of God, music that is not of God, magazines that are not of God, websites that are not of God, hanging around people that don't care about God, then I will desire things that are not of God.

So, how do I daily win this battle of sinful nature vs. the Spirit? The answer is simple: I need to rely on the strength of Jesus (Phil. 4:13) and I need to fill up my time with the things of God (the right things), then I will desire God.

Romans 8:5
"Live according to sin nature, your mind will be set on what that nature desires...those who live according to the Spirit, your mind will be set on what the Spirit desires."

Galatians 6:7-8
"Do not be deceived: God cannot be mocked. A man reaps what he sows. The one who sows to please his sinful nature, from that nature will reap destruction; the one who sows to please the Spirit, from the Spirit will reap eternal life."

As I fill up my mind with the things of God, I will want more and more of Him. I won't desire what the world has to offer, but I will want God and the things of God.

Galatians 5:16
"...live by the Spirit, and you will not gratify the desires of the sinful nature."

My goal as a Christian is to stay on the green line and invite others to hop on the green line with me. Daily, I must continue to SEEK after Jesus. I need to continually walk with Jesus and keep in step with Jesus until I reach the finish line.

Galatians 5:25
"Since we live by the Spirit, let us keep in step with the Spirit."

What does your life look like? Circle the actions that most describe you this past year?

 a. *"The following are acts of sinful nature: "sexual immorality, impurity and debauchery [corruptness],, idolatry and witchcraft, hatred, discord, jealousy, fits of rage, selfish ambition, dissension, factions and envy; drunkenness, orgies, and the like…"* (Galatians 5:19-21)

 b. *"…love, joy, peace, patience, kindness, goodness, faithfulness, gentleness, and self-control…clothe yourselves with compassion, kindness, humility gentleness and patience."* (Galatians 5:22-23, Colossians 3:12)

If the first paragraph has more circles, then you've most likely been living for yourself and not striving to stay on the green line. If you have more circles in the second paragraph then you most likely are on the green line and please God. Our actions, our thought life, and our motives are a direct reflection of who is winning the battle of sin nature vs. the Spirit.

Another test is to fill out your daily schedule. This chart will reveal where and with whom you've spent most of your time. Again, if God is not a focus throughout the day, then there is a good chance that your mind is getting filled up with worldly things.

Sun	Mon	Tues	Wed	Thurs	Fri	Sat

My challenge to you today is simple: spend more time with things pleasing to God rather than the things of this world and you will remain on the GREEN line!

———✂———

2 *UNDERSTAND GOSPEL VERSES:*

Romans 10:9-10 - That if you confess with your mouth, "Jesus is Lord," and believe in your heart that God raised him from the dead, you will be saved. For it is with your heart that you believe and are justified, and it is with your mouth that you confess and are saved.

③ *IMPROVE LEADERSHIP SKILLS:*

Read the following sentence taken from a witnessing tract:

FINISHED FILES ARE THE RESULT OF YEARS OF SCIENTIFIC STUDY COMBINED WITH THE EXPERIENCE OF YEARS.

Now, count the number of F's in the sentence (Count them only once).

How many F's do you count?

The answer: Although there are 6 F's in the above statement, most people count 3 or 4. This is because they read the sentence too quickly and skip the F's in the word "of."

Application:

When you move too quickly through life, you'll most likely miss the details. Our eyes often deceive us. Some of the details that you may miss may be very important. Make sure to take your time and not rush through life. Pay attention to the details so that you don't miss out on opportunities God has set before you!

—✕—

④ *LEARN LEADERSHIP PRINCIPLES:*

I'm part of the fellowship of the unashamed. I have Holy Spirit power. The die has been cast. I have stepped over the line. The decision has been made. I'm a disciple of His. I won't look back, let up, slow down, or back away. My past is redeemed, my present makes sense; my future is secure. I'm finished and done with low living, tamed visions, mundane talking, cheap giving, and dwarfed goals. I no longer need pre-eminence, prosperity, position, or popularity. I don't have to be recognized, praised, regarded or rewarded. I now live by faith, lean on His presence, walk by patience, lift by prayer and labor by power. My face is set, my gait is fast, my goal is heaven, my road is narrow, my way is rough, my companions few, my guide reliable, my mission clear. I cannot be bought, compromised, detoured, lured away, turned back, deluded or delayed. I will not flinch in the face of sacrifice, hesitate in the presence of procrastination, negotiate at the table of fear, ponder at the pool of popularity, or meander in the maze of mediocrity.

I won't give up, shut up, let up until I've stayed up, stored up, prayed up, and paid up, for the cause of Christ. I am a disciple of Jesus. I must go till He comes, give till I drop, and witness till all know. And when He comes for His own, He will have no problem recognizing me - my banner will be clear. I am a fruit-bearing servant of Jesus Christ!

- Author Unknown

—✕—

❺ *DEVELOP TEAM UNITY:*

Cheetos:

Hand out a Cheeto to every team member and instruct them to hold it during the entire lesson for today. Be prepared that the students will complain, but encourage them that there is a point to this!

At the end of the lesson, tell the students to throw the Cheeto away or eat it. At this point, their fingertips should be orange from holding the Cheeto for so long. Even when they try and wash their hands, a little orange remains for a time after.

Tell the students that just like the orange stain on their fingers produced from the Cheeto, scars that remain are produced from impurity.

Hold a Cheeto in your hand, by the end it leaves your fingers scarred with orange...just like impurities! Impurities can be forgiven but most of the time will leave scars that will remain for a long time.

Application:

Seek God and pursue holiness and receive God's blessings instead of Satan's scars.

PRACTICAL QUESTIONS/ANSWERS

Before we get into some practical questions and answers, both Jon and I want to applaud you for investing in the next generation at the leadership level! We are living in a time where babysitting students is not good enough. Entertaining students with the latest tech craze will not cut it. Attracting large crowds, for the sake of validating how successful you are as a youth pastor, will not lead to a God sized movement that transforms a culture.

So, we want to thank you for choosing to build student leaders who will multiply the discipleship initiative. We want to thank you for choosing to invest in students and lead them through a spiritual growth process that will lead to consistent Godly fruit that is not just a phase.

Students need us, as youth leaders, to keep believing in them. They need us to keep cheering them on. They need us to keep caring about their world. If we don't, who else will? Who else will point them to Jesus? Who else will equip them to follow Jesus? Who else will give them opportunities to experience life serving Jesus? Who else will enlarge their level of influence and provide opportunities to grow as a leader?

God bless you and your family as you answer God's call to invest in the leaders of today and tomorrow. God bless you and your ministry as you try and stay focused and keep the main thing the main thing. God bless you as you try to reach families for the Gospel through students. God bless you as you try and transform schools for the cause of Christ through students. God bless you as you try to lead by example and correctly juggle all that is coming at you.

We would love to interact with you. If you get a chance, visit our website www.EquipStudentLeaders.com for more resources and our contact information. To get started in our interaction, continue reading through the following question and answer section and we look forward to connecting with you soon!

WHY HAVE A STUDENT LEADERSHIP TEAM?

1. Jesus chose to invest in and equip 12 men to change the world. Likewise, choosing to invest in and equip student leaders can change your culture.

2. It allows the student pastor/director to multiply himself/herself into students who want to be challenged at the next level.

3. It creates an organized opportunity for students to grow and apply at the leadership level, thus intentionally impacting all grade levels and all ministry environments.

TIPS FOR A SUCCESSFUL LEADERSHIP TEAM: HOW SHOULD I GET STARTED?

1. Advertise and have student leadership applications available (example in resources section).

2. Recruit a highly trusted adult selection team (Student Pastor/Director makes final decisions).

3. Contact the selected students and invite to a Leadership Launch Event.

4. Begin regularly meeting and working through this curriculum.

WHEN SHOULD I GET STARTED?

1. Promote the leadership opportunity at the end of the school year for students to pray and think about applying for over the summer.

2. Allow for at least three weeks to promote and hand out the application in August.

3. Make the selections and host a Leadership Launch Event to kick off the student leadership program just before Labor Day or a week after Labor Day. At this event, provide team members and parents with materials about the program, the goals for the program, and resources available to the student leaders (include anything and everything unique to the student leadership team: mission trip dates, fun trip dates, meeting dates, goals and strategies, other student leader programs and resources like Student Leadership University, etc.). Bring in a guest speaker to challenge and motivate the students and parents in relation to leadership and their task to lead that year.

WHAT IS THE TARGET AGE GROUP FOR A STUDENT LEADERSHIP TEAM?

Middle School: 8th Grade Year

High School: 11th and 12th Grade years

HOW OFTEN SHOULD THE GROUP MEET?

1. At least two times a month throughout the year.

2. Include at least one or two fun trips (one per semester) with the purpose of getting the team together.

3. Include a mission opportunity for the team to serve on together.

What are some goals to accomplish at the leadership meetings?

1. Work through a spiritual growth curriculum that covers the foundations of living the Christian life (The curriculum in this notebook will give you a great start with an emphasis on leadership.).

2. Provide a Gospel-focused memory verse.

3. Teach a practical leadership lesson.

4. Provide a Leadership Quote.

5. Complete a team building exercise.

WHAT DOES AN EXAMPLE YEAR LOOK LIKE?

August:

Promote/Provide Student Leader Applications
Select student leaders
Possible Leadership Launch Event

September:

Possible Leadership Launch Event
Begin 2 * Month meetings

October:

2 * Month meetings
Fun trip

November:

2 * Month meetings

December:

2 * Month meetings

January:

2 * Month meetings
Accept applications again for those that didn't make it the first time, but worked toward improving.

February:

2 * Month meetings
Complete 12 sessions

March:

2 * Month meetings
Fun trip
Prepare students for Leadership Month

April:

2 * Month meetings
Prepare students for Leadership Month

May:

2 * Month meetings (mission trip training)
Leadership Month (student leaders teach small groups one
week, students speak at large group gatherings, students give
testimonials, etc.)

June:

Student Leadership Mission Trip

July:

Student Leadership Get-a-way (reflect on the past year,
commission off into the next year)

HOW DO I PREPARE MY STUDENT LEADERS TO TEACH A SMALL GROUP CLASS?

Pick a day during the year to allow your students to teach
a Bible lesson to other students. Allow for at least a month
of preparation. Group the students up in groups of 2-4
students so that they can prepare for the lesson together.
Make sure that each student in the teaching group is active
and involved. Have the students choose which teaching
structure (listed below) that they would like to use and
weekly check in with them. Challenge them to create enough

material for at least a 45 minute lesson. Remind them that being a teacher of God's Word is an awesome responsibility so they need to take it very seriously.

Teaching structures (not original to the authors):

HBLT - DOES MY LESSON HAVE STRUCTURE?

Hook: Introduction, draws audience in. Variety of ways to do this.
Book: Bible teaching should focus on a big idea.
Look: Implication, So What? Why does this passage apply to the students?
Took: Application, Now What? How can I put this into practice?

Example: Romans 12:1-2

Hook: (Introduction) Have students define worship on the white board. Discuss what worship looks like in church today. How was worship different 2,000 years ago?

Book: (Lesson) Three Facets of Worship (Romans 12:1-2)
1. Offer your body as a living sacrifice.
2. Do not conform to the patterns of this world.
3. Be transformed by the renewing of your mind.

Look: (Implications) So What? Do you worship God merely on Sundays? Do you worship God daily? If so, how? What does a living sacrifice look like?

Took: (Applications) Now What? This week, do one nice thing for a stranger each day. Write down what you did, the person's response, and how you felt. We'll discuss at the beginning of next week's class.

CAR - DOES MY LESSON ANSWER THESE QUESTIONS?

Clear: Can my lesson be restated in a sentence?

Accurate: Does my lesson accurately depict
truth from Scripture?

Relevant: Does my lesson apply to my audience today?

VOTE - DOES MY LESSON FLOW LOGICALLY? DOES MY LESSON INSPIRE?

Vision: What is my purpose or goal?
* The focus of the lesson.

Obstruction: What obstacles get in the way of
reaching my goal?
* Problem keeping me from accomplishing
the big idea.

Transformation: How can I change to reach my goal?
* How can God change me, or what should
be different?

Enlist: What steps can I take today to help reach my goal?
* Give practical, directional, and applicable steps.

AN INTERVIEW WITH NATHAN WILDER AND JON KRAGEL:

1. What is your current church and position?

Nathan Wilder: "Minister of Students and Sports Outreach"
Jon Kragel: "Minister of High School Students"

2. What has been your first-hand experience on the benefits of having a student leadership team?

"We have experienced countless benefits to a student leadership team. At our church, we have an 8th Grade Student Leadership Team as well as an 11th and 12th Grade Student Leadership Team. We invest in these students twice a month on average and it is worth the investment! These students become a team and grow into a family as they help us lead our worship service environment, our small group environment, our ministry team environment, and our mission trip environment. These students are also the first ones that we recruit from to help with church wide ministry events as well. We've just performed a study and found that 96% of our Student Leaders were regularly involved in church after graduating from High School. The bottom line is that it has been invaluable to have a team of students who are ready and trustworthy to be the church now and in the future!"

3. What are some of the ways that the students lead?

"Our student leadership teams help us lead in our worship environment, our small group environment, our ministry team environment, and our mission trip environment. We also dedicate the month of May as Leadership Month. During this month, our student leaders take over and have the opportunity to preach, lead small groups, and execute a big evangelistic event."

4. How has the Equip Material been beneficial to raising up student leaders?

"We have used the Equip Book material for our 8th Grade Leadership Teams over the past 7 years. We have found it to be very user friendly for the students and as a result they have been able to reproduce it to disciple a student or group of students. It is our hope that they hold on to this foundational information so that they can continue to build on it as they grow older and as they mature spiritually."

5. Are you currently building a team? If so, at what point in the process are you?

"We built the Student Leadership Team structure about 7 years ago and now have it established enough for parents and students to know all that they can expect for the year that they serve on student leadership. In a ministry of 200 middle school students and 200 high school students, on average we see about 30 8th grade leaders per year and about 45 11th and 12th graders selected and make the commitment to be on the leadership team."

FURTHER RESOURCES:

"Visit www.EquipStudentLeaders.com to interact with the authors as well as find more resources on the subject of building student leaders, student leadership teams, and multiplying disciples."

ABOUT THE AUTHORS

NATHAN WILDER BIO

Rev. Nathan Wilder is a native of Florida and has been
married to his beautiful wife, Amber, since 2002. They have
4 amazing children, Reese, Macey, Lexie and Daisy. Nathan
joined the staff at FBC Oviedo, FL in January 2006 and
currently oversees Elevate High School Ministry, Emerge
Middle School Ministry, and Sports Outreach Ministry. He
received a Master of Science degree from Florida State
University, a Master of Education degree from Liberty
University, and a Master of Divinity degree from Liberty
University. He is currently working on his Doctorate from
Liberty University. Nathan is a contributing author in *Impact:
The Student Leadership Devotional*, and his ministry has been
highlighted as successful case studies in the book *Simple
Student Ministry.*

—✳—

JON KRAGEL BIO

Rev. Jon Kragel has been married to his incredible wife,
Samantha, since 2006. Together, they have two sons, Jackson
and Carter. Jon currently serves as the Minister to High
School Students at First Baptist Church Oviedo, located in
central Florida. Jon has a Bachelor of Arts from Cedarville
University and a Masters of Divinity from Liberty Baptist
Theological Seminary. Jon is a contributing author in *Impact:
The Student Leadership Devotional*, and two of his youth
ministries have been highlighted as successful case studies in
the book *Simple Student Ministry.*

www.ingramcontent.com/pod-product-compliance
Lightning Source LLC
LaVergne TN
LVHW011333080426
835513LV00006B/327